DEDICATION:

This guide was written by Peter Tobin, part of the mrbruff.com team. The
Tobin. Thank you, Peter, for your excessive hard work.

A big thank you must go to Sam Perkins and Sunny Ratilal, who between them designed
cover of this guide. Sunny designed the original template which I used for previous books, and Sam
adapted it for this text. Both are hugely talented.

Thanks once again to Joan Waters, who gave up endless hours to proofread this text.

MW00397454

Contents

Introduction to the Second Edition

Readers may wonder why there's a need for an updated edition of a revision guide based on a play that's over 400 years old. Hasn't it all been said already? It's just over five years since the first edition of *Mr Bruff's Guide to Macbeth* was published and we now have a great deal of information and feedback from exam boards and exam reports, as well as exam questions from the last three years of GCSE exams.

Overall, it's clear that the exam boards want to see students taking a more holistic approach to the text. Rather than simply technique spotting, they want students to engage with the big ideas in the text and to understand the text both in the context from which it arises but also the context of the modern audience. This means that students need to understand the text as being deliberately created by the writer, to view the characters as constructs. It also asks students to think about what the writer wanted the audience to understand after watching the play.

None of this is easy considering the play is over 400 years old and we can't know with any degree of certainty what message Shakespeare wanted his audience to leave the theatre with. There is, however, a way of contextualising *Macbeth* and Shakespeare's other plays, a way of framing them that allow us to see his characters, particularly Macbeth himself, in a fuller light. One part of the play where this idea is made is clear is in Act 5 Scene 8 when a seemingly small exchange between two minor characters may highlight Shakespeare's attitude.

When Macduff secures Malcolm's help to remove Macbeth from the throne, they also gain the support of some noble lords from England, one of whom is Siward. Siward, known in some copies of the play as Old Siward because his son is also part of the battle, is told by Ross that his son is dead. Ross announces to Siward that "Your son, my lord, has paid a soldier's debt" and Siward's reply is to ask "Had he his hurts before?" implying that if he had had his wounds on his back, it would suggest he had been running away from the fight. When he learns that his son had his wounds to his front, then Siward is happy and says "I would not wish him a fairer death: And so, his knell is knoll'd".

Malcolm, soon-to-be king, interjects and says "He's worth more sorrow, And that I'll spend for him." But here, Siward says something interesting about his son: he says "He's worth no more". This is a surprising thing for a grieving father to say about his deceased son only moments after learning of his death but it tells us a lot about the environment and the world of the play and also the Elizabethan and Jacobean worlds Shakespeare lived in. Siward is happy to accept the death of his son because he "paid a soldier's death". This was his job, his role in the system. He was there to fight on behalf of the rightful king. His job, as it were, was to be willing to die on behalf of Malcolm. That was his place in the system of how the world worked. That he did that well (his wounds were to his front) is all that Siward needs to know. Shakespeare is reinforcing here the importance of tradition and the system as it exists and the roles that people play within that system.

In 1543 Copernicus proposed the radical idea that the earth wasn't the centre of the universe as previously thought but in fact that the sun was the centre of our universe and that the earth, like the other planets, rotated around it. In 1517 The Reformation, a religious movement that resulted in the splintering of Christianity into Catholicism and Protestantism, had undermined the authority of the pope and the church as a whole. For Shakespeare (whose parents were supposedly Catholics), he lives at a time when the certainties of life – God, the universe and our place in it – were being questioned and the development of individual will – Humanism and Individualism – were becoming more concrete.

According to the critic G.K. Hunter, the central issue of Elizabethan intellectual life was the theological debate about the relation of individual conscience to the established hierarchies of the world. In other words, Elizabethans (not all, but particularly the educated ones) were wondering where they fit in in the grand scheme of things. A contemporary of Shakespeare's – Christopher Marlowe – wrote a play called *Tamburlaine the Great* in 1587, a play Shakespeare would most definitely have seen and admired which dealt with some controversial themes and ideas. The central character, Tamburlaine, rises from being a lowly shepherd to being the ruler of an enormous kingdom through his own actions – God is not given credit for his success. This highlights the idea of the individual being able to have an impact upon the world through their own ideas, thoughts and actions. To the Elizabethans who believed that everyone's position in the world, the great chain of being, was fixed, this was shockingly radical. Even Robert Greene, a contemporary of both Marlowe and Shakespeare, praised the play for its writing but condemned it for being "atheist".

So, Shakespeare is living and writing at a time when the world is changing. Things are less certain and this lack of certainty prompts a number of different responses form a variety of playwrights. Nashe and Greene simply complain and describe Shakespeare as a thief, an impersonator and a low-educated entertainer. Marlowe reacts by focusing on the primacy and power of the individual, not just a person in a system like a cog in a wheel. Critics describe Tamburlaine as rising from nothing and his rapid accumulation of power is entirely created by his individual ambition and will. Shakespeare, however, takes a different path.

In his article *The Beginnings of Elizabethan Drama: Revolution and Continuity*, the critic G.K. Hunter maintains that during the 100 years that would have comprised Shakespeare's life – roughly the 1530s to the 1640s – there was a constant effort to keep the prevailing system in place. That included loyalty to the crown, to the country, to the church as well as to the existing traditions. This was achieved through keeping order and punishing those who deviated from the accepted system. For example, those who were believed to be involved in the Gunpowder Plot to assassinate King James I were executed. Their reasons for the plot were not explored or debated. Peter Ackroyd argues in his book *Shakespeare: The Biography* that Shakespeare was a defender and supporter of royal power. He in no way would have supported any popular movements to give power to the people and often ridiculed and mocked those in the lower classes for their illiteracy.

Macbeth in particular is a conservative and orthodox play. It has been suggested by many that it was written for King James I because of the focus on the witches at the beginning (King James I wrote a book on the subject called *Daemonologie* and was known to be fascinated by it), it is set in Scotland (King James's birthplace) and it deals with the downfall of someone who kills a king to usurp the crown (it was written in the same year as the failure of the Gunpowder Plot). All of these factors imply that Shakespeare wrote the play to curry favour with the King. And why wouldn't he? Shakespeare and the company of actors that he worked with had previously been known as Lord Chamberlain's Men and now their title changed to the King's Men. This meant Shakespeare was a servant of the Royal Court and his social status was greatly improved. It also meant that his work had a very particular outlook on royalty, the divine right of kings and the great chain of being. As Ackroyd points out, Shakespeare was an apologist for royal power. None of his titular characters are lowborn. He was fascinated with the idea of kingship and power and exploring characters of high status. It's even said that in performances with the Lord Chamberlain's men, Shakespeare himself often played the role of kings.

And so, we come to the idea of what his message could be. There is always the potential that he simply didn't have one and there are some critics who believe this to be the case. It's clear that his purpose, his aim, was to entertain and he achieved that with all of his plays. In terms of his message, I can't help but think that he was reaffirming the status quo, sticking to traditional, conservative values and concerns. Shakespeare was, financially, very clever and never got himself into the sort of trouble that his contemporaries often did. When attacked in pamphlets by fellow playwrights, he never responded, only sometimes making fun of them in his plays. We begin to get a picture of a man who very much avoids taking risks where possible. He doesn't do anything that will make waves or get himself into any trouble with the Master of Revels (like the modern-day censorship board) , his contemporaries or even the theatre-going public.

So his message could have been just that. That on the brink of the great changes in Elizabethan society, the shift in values, in religious outlook and even in how people saw their place in the universe, Shakespeare was cautioning against a full departure from the system they lived and worked in. It benefitted him greatly, why would he want to change it?

Ultimately it's impossible to know for certain what message Shakespeare wanted his audience to leave the theatre with and all we can do as students and teachers is infer from the evidence available. The exam boards have made clear that, whatever a student's interpretation is, it needs to be grounded in both context and a thorough understanding of the text and its characters. The subsequent chapters will give some more information about stagecraft (how the play is performed in the stage) and the characters and how we can understand their functions in the world of the play.

One final note is on the usage of the terms 'Elizabethan' and 'Jacobean' to describe the times in which Shakespeare lived and wrote. Queen Elizabeth's reign, the Elizabethan era, was from 1558 to 1603 while the Jacobean era, the reign of King James I, lasted from 1603 to 1625. Shakespeare himself lived from 1564 to 1616. It's clear that Shakespeare's formative years were during the Elizabethan era. This is when his views and ideas were formed and when he started out in his career as a playwright. *Macbeth* itself, however, was written and first performed in the Jacobean era. In this guide, the terms will often be used together to refer to a shared attitude or perspective as there was little immediate change from the end of one era to the beginning of the other. When speaking specifically about *Macbeth*, students should use the term 'Jacobean'.

Stagecraft

It is often forgotten that *Macbeth* is a play. So much so that examiner's reports regularly point this fact out. Students need to remember that Macbeth was written to be performed, not to be read. When we think about the play from the perspective of its roots, we get a fuller understanding of what Shakespeare was trying to achieve. Writing in the early 17th Century, Shakespeare needed to achieve one thing more than anything else – he needed to entertain his audience.

The Globe theatre, the theatre Shakespeare and the other members of his company of actors, The King's Men, owned, could hold thousands. Without the benefit of microphones and speakers and other modern conveniences, Shakespeare had to make sure that his play held the attention of thousands of paying customers. There would have been all types of people watching *Macbeth* when it was first performed, from the poor and illiterate of London to the upper-class people of the professional classes. How did Shakespeare ensure that he kept them coming back?

Late Elizabethan and early Jacobean theatre was gaining a reputation for the spectacular – stunning sets and stage machinery as well as costumes, music, dancing and visual symbolism were all a part of theatre around the time *Macbeth* was first performed. Similarly, it has been said that there were fifty-nine different gestures of the hands to signify different moods and states of minds within the characters. This was obviously important as, at times, people may not have even been able to hear what was happening. There was a fine tradition of the audience participating to the point where they often drowned out the actors' voices!

The acting, too, would have been rather different from today. Nowadays we expect realism when we go to the theatre whereas the Elizabethans would not have expected anything of the sort. The acting would have been expressive, what we today might call over the top and the aim was to communicate to the audience the depth of feeling and emotion that was being experienced on stage.

Aside from the visual power of costumes and props, however, there has to be something deeper in Shakespeare's work that made his plays so powerful and made his theatre the one that people kept flocking to. Many other theatres in London at the time had access to similar costumes and similar props and there were many other playwrights working in London too. Shakespeare's advantage is that he was able to portray a world, in the case of *Macbeth*, 11th century Scotland, in a convincing way that kept audiences engaged from beginning to end.

It is a feature of Shakespeare's drama that he creates a world that is already in process. We often feel, as the audience, like we are eavesdropping or almost intruding on the lives of the characters on the stage. This is evident in *Macbeth* from the very beginning. The play begins and the three witches are almost finished whatever they were doing before we 'arrive' saying "when shall we three meet again". Whatever they were doing, it is already complete. Shakespeare creates a world that is already in motion.

It's also interesting to note that the majority of Shakespeare's plays were written without acts. In most of the plays, the acts were put in afterwards when more indoor theatres were being built and they had the ability to change scenery and move actors on and off stage. Without these divisions, the action would have been constant. The actors would be entering from an ongoing world which is fully alive in some other place. The action that we see on stage, then, is an intense, focussed episode within that larger world of the play and Shakespeare sequences these episodes so well that the sequence itself seems life-like or to mimic real life.

Macbeth in particular proceeds at a quick pace. It is one of the shortest of Shakespeare's plays and the action is intense. From the beginning to the end, the play is like a thriller. The narrative pushes us forward at an ever-quickening pace. To aid this, Shakespeare depicts events in Macbeth proceeding one after another with very little extra material. After she receives her husband's letter in Act 1 Scene 5, Lady Macbeth is already determined to see her plan through. She doesn't hesitate and doesn't waste words in trying to convince anyone. Even when she is persuading Macbeth himself, she does this with great economy of words. It is 14 lines from when he says "we shall proceed no further in this business" to when he admits defeat with "If we should fail".

Similarly, Shakespeare makes use of a rhetorical device called stichomythia where characters use very brief sentences but these sentences are linked to each other. This quickens the pace of the dialogue and, therefore, increases the speed at which the action unfolds for the audience. For example, in Act 2 Scene 2 after Macbeth returns from murdering Duncan, the rapid alternation in dialogue between Macbeth and Lady Macbeth increases the pace of the action and the tension for the reader:

Macbeth:
I have done the deed. Didst thou not hear a noise?

Lady Macbeth:
I heard the owl scream and the crickets cry.
Did you not speak?

Macbeth:
When?

Lady Macbeth:
Now.

Macbeth:
As I descended?

Lady Macbeth:
Ay.

There are many considerations for why we don't see such things as Macbeth's coronation as King or the murder of Duncan. In one sense, the play isn't about his coronation and the pomp and ceremony that would entail. Similarly, the play is not necessarily about the physical violence involved in murder but instead the psychological impact of being king, of having committed murder. Macbeth's crimes take place offstage or are undertaken by other people but the reactions to them are vividly present on stage in his soliloquies and in his interactions with Lady Macbeth.

It's also been said that, because of the lack of acts within his plays, the entrances and exits within Shakespeare's plays, and again, *Macbeth* in particular, are crucial. When we examine the entrances and exits in Macbeth, they are a key part of how the action and drama is increased from beginning to end. After Duncan reports that he has been betrayed, who enters? Macbeth. There's also the clever switching of focus throughout much of Act 5. We move from Macbeth's castle to the approaching forces and back again repeatedly, building towards the final climax.

So, Shakespeare's choices in terms of what he shows on stage and what he doesn't is all part of his awareness of stagecraft. Similarly, the use of the witches at the beginning, and the deployment of

Banquo's ghost during the Banquet scene are all markers of a playwright who knew exactly what his audience wanted to see.

Macbeth

The character of Macbeth may be understood in a number of different ways. On the first level, we can see Macbeth as a character who is destroyed by having too much ambition. He is already a thane, he is the King's most trusted general and yet he is not happy. He wants the crown for himself and all it takes is a prophecy from the "weird sisters" to set him off. In pursuing that ambition, he ends up destroying himself, his family, everything. To look at Macbeth in this way is to take Shakespeare's message to be a warning of the dangers of being over ambitious.

"Brave Macbeth" to a "dead butcher"

Shakespeare makes it clear the impact that this surplus of ambition has on Macbeth. At the beginning, he is portrayed as a brave, noble warrior. He is described as "brave Macbeth", by the Bloody Sergeant and "valiant cousin, worthy gentleman" by King Duncan in Act 1 Scene 2 but over the course of the play he changes completely so that by the end, in Act 5 Scene 8 the epithet Malcolm uses to describe him is "dead butcher". He undergoes a transformation from Act 1 to Act 5 and we see this play out before our very eyes. Macbeth wants to be king, he is aware of the ambition within him. In Act 1 Scene 7 he says, "I have no spur to prick the sides of my intent but only vaulting ambition…". Here he acknowledges that there's no reason for him to kill Duncan but his own ambition. There is a remarkable passage before this quote where he goes through all of the reasons why he *shouldn't* kill the king. Shakespeare is painting a picture of a man who is at war with himself. He has the ambition within him but logic and reason, his own mind, is telling him not to do it.

Predictably, after Macbeth carries out the murder, he begins to suffer the consequences almost immediately. He is frightened and rambling in his speech when he tries to speak with his wife, a direct contrast with the experienced and skilled warrior on the battlefield described in Act 1 Scene 2 and the well-spoken, eloquent Macbeth we see just one scene earlier. He believes that he has "murdered sleep" and even heard a voice call out that "Macbeth shall sleep no more". When we consider sleep as a symbol of peace of mind, it's clear that Shakespeare is showing us that Macbeth's deeds, in the name of ambition, have destroyed his conscience and he will no longer have peace of mind. He has destroyed that part of himself. This is clearly a huge price to pay for an ambitious nature and many people have interpreted this as Shakespeare's warning about the cost of being over ambitious.

Another consequence of Macbeth's actions is his descent into blood and further murders. It's a path that he cannot turn back on once he has begun and he makes this clear in Act 3 Scene 4 when he says "blood will have blood". The spilling of blood simply leads to more blood being spilt. Later in the same scene, Macbeth says, "I am in blood stepped in so far, that, should I wade no more, returning were as tedious as go o'er." This is a poignant image of Macbeth, wading through a river of blood and realising that he may as well keep going as returning to what he was before. Again, Shakespeare is showing the consequences of unchecked ambition.

Ultimately, Macbeth undergoes a brief revival at the end of the play. For this play to be a tragedy, the main protagonist or central character must be a tragic hero and fall from a high position (socially) because of some tragic flaw (hamartia) within themselves. In *Macbeth*, the main protagonist decides to kill the king to fulfill his ambitions and this leads to his downfall. These elements of tragedy and the tragic hero stem from Aristotle's *Poetics* and were developed by the critic A.C. Bradley to further explore Shakespeare's tragedies and tragic heroes in particular. In order to fit the mould of a tragic hero then, it's important that Shakespeare creates some sympathy for Macbeth, some re-establishing of his former glory before he dies. He does this through showing Macbeth in Act 5 deciding to fight against the invading English army despite the fact that he is woefully outnumbered and destined to fail. It is this bravery, in the face of certain defeat that restores Macbeth in some people's eyes to his former glory. It is very difficult, as a modern audience, to ignore all of Macbeth's evil deeds throughout the course of the play but, if you consider it from an Elizabethan and Jacobean perspective, there is glory in his refusal to give in and allow "the rabble" to bait him. He is noble after all and not a commoner and his line in Act 5 Scene 5, "Blow, wind! Come, wrack! At least we'll die with harness on our back" is fitting of a tragic hero.

Aside from seeing the play *Macbeth* as a cautionary tale about the dangers of ambition, there are other ways of looking at the character of Macbeth, especially if we consider Shakespeare's intentions when writing the play. As we know from the Introduction, the play was written in the same year that the Gunpowder Plot (a plot to assassinate King James I) was foiled. Shakespeare, as one of the King's Men and a servant to the court, wrote a play that supports the traditions and the established hierarchies of the court and the crown. As you will remember from the introduction also, Shakespeare was writing at a time of change when ideas about authority, rules and man's place within the world were changing. From this perspective, we can see Macbeth as an example of what happens when you try to take fate into your own hands and go against the chain of being and established order.

Macbeth, as a Thane and one of Duncan's most trusted generals, has a very privileged position. Generally, the crown passed down to a King's eldest son. In Scotland, as a consequence of bloody wars, there was an exception made and a King was allowed to choose his successor – it didn't have to be his son. Macbeth expects Duncan to choose him and, when he doesn't, plots to kill him. Shakespeare is writing the play in support of the monarchy and in support of the idea of Kingship and so, he makes an example of Macbeth and shows what happens when you step outside of your pre-ordained role within society. Macbeth has contravened the established rules and traditions. He is not being loyal to his king or his country, he is simply being loyal to his own ambition, something that Shakespeare cannot condone.

Looking at Macbeth in this light, we see that all the things that befall him are the consequences of his individualism and his selfishness. In Act 3 Scene 4 he says, "for mine own good / All causes shall give way". Life, Shakespeare appears to be saying, has meaning only within the roles decided for us by god and, by extension, the King. Macbeth cannot be happy once he steps outside his position. To go against the establishment for selfish individualism is to open the door to chaos, evil and, ultimately, death.

Finally, another way to look at the character of Macbeth is as an exploration of masculinity. We have, at the beginning, the presentation of Macbeth in stereotypically masculine terms. He is described as "carving" his way through the men on the battlefield and "unseaming" the rebel lord, Macdonwald. Macbeth is powerful, warrior-like and manly. The closeness exhibited with his wife in the letter she reads in Act 1 Scene 5 as well as the dominance she shows in their subsequent scenes together changes the picture somewhat. How can Macbeth be presented as a warrior on one hand and yet almost afraid of his wife on the other?
His reluctance to kill the king, indecision before the act and his suffering afterwards are all signs of his weakness or as Lady Macbeth puts it, his excess of "human kindness". So within Macbeth there are two types of masculinity. The stereotypical one that surrounds ideas of violence and cruelty. When Lady Macbeth asks the spirits to "unsex her" and fill her with "direst cruelty" it's so that she

can be manly enough to kill Duncan. When Macbeth is trying to encourage the murderers to kill Banquo, they respond with "we are men my liege".

When Macbeth is trying to fend off his wife's bullying he says "I dare do all that may become a man" and when Lady Macbeth is trying to goad her husband into killing Duncan, she attacks his manhood: "Are you a man?" and "When you durst do it, then you were a man". And the other type of masculinity that is rational, kind and decent. This is exhibited when Macbeth lists the reasons he shouldn't kill the King. Chief among them is that he is a man, not simply that he is the king. We also see this side of Macbeth in his closeness with his wife as well as his regrets in Act 5.

Macbeth then is torn between these competing types of masculinity. He eventual goes against the kindness in his own heart and resorts to the stereotypical presentation of masculinity and this ends up being his downfall.

Lady Macbeth

Like her husband, there are multiple ways of interpreting the character of Lady Macbeth. She too changes over the course of the play from her presentation in Act 1 as a fiercely malevolent force, intent on convincing her husband to do her bidding no matter what the consequences, to a broken and defeated woman in Act 5 who is tortured by her own guilt and her inability to find peace of mind.

Again, like with Macbeth, the underlying message from Shakespeare may be one of the dangers of ambition. She is reduced from a seemingly powerful character to a mere shadow in the space of five acts. Here there is also a telling reference in *Holinshed's Chronicles,* Shakespeare's source material for the play. *Holinshed's Chronicles* was a history book with which many people would have been familiar and in it there is the re-telling of the true story of *King Macbeth of Scotland, Macduff and Duncan.* The play itself differs in some details from the real-life Macbeth but there may be a hint in the Gaelic nickname he had, Ri Deircc, which translates as "the red king". In *Holinshed's Chronicles*, there is also a reference to an ambition-crazed queen who Shakespeare, no doubt, based his Lady Macbeth on. If Macbeth is in any doubt about whether or not he should proceed with the plan to kill Duncan, Lady Macbeth doesn't flinch for a second. From the moment she reads her husband's letter regarding the prophecy, she is hell-bent on seeing it through.

There is even an interesting point In Act 1 Scene 5 when, having read the letter, a servant enters the scene and says, "The king comes here tonight." Having allowed her mind to rush ahead, she says "Thou art mad to say it" indicating that she has, momentarily, thought the servant was referring to her husband and not Duncan, who is still very much alive. So, we can assume then that Lady Macbeth is just as ambitious as her husband. Considering the restrictions that many women faced in Elizabethan and Jacobean times and considering further that the play is set in the 11th century, it's clear that Lady Macbeth needs her husband in order to realise her own ambitions of being queen. She is, in a sense, using him to fulfil her own desires.

Many people argue that Shakespeare was proto-feminist. Seeing as feminism ,as it exists today, did not exist in the 16th century, we use 'proto' at the beginning in order to make that distinction. Scholars often look at his female characters and point to their eloquence and strength of character when they say that Shakespeare must have been sending some sort of message about women and what he thought of them.

There is some truth in that idea Lady Macbeth is a striking character. She dominates her husband in a wholly subversive way. It goes against much of what we know about gender roles in Elizabethan and Jacobean England. Even for Lady Macbeth to have the desire to be queen recognises her not simply as a woman or a wife but as an individual with desires and ambitions. As a small, but significant aside, approximately 90% of all women in Shakespeare's time were illiterate yet Lady Macbeth is not. Our very first introduction to her sees her reading a letter. Granted she is a high-born character but it's significant nonetheless. Another point is that when Macbeth speaks to his wife he uses phrases such as "dearest partner" and "dearest chuck" perhaps suggesting that he sees his wife as his equal. Whereas when she speaks to him, she refers to his titles – "worthy Cawdor..." Perhaps Lady Macbeth is a powerful, almost evil character who is using whatever is at her disposal in order to achieve what she most desperately craves: power.

But another way of looking at Lady Macbeth is to consider her as not powerful at all, that she is, in fact weak and that far from being a proto-feminist, Shakespeare is actually depicting Lady Macbeth as weak and powerless and typical of a woman of her time. Lady Macbeth is ambitious but she needs the help and support of the forces of darkness in order to carry out her plan. Following the killing, she is terrified. Perhaps this scene is the true picture of Lady Macbeth as it is the one that we see in Act 5 also when she is sleepwalking. She has become a mere shadow; she has faded into insignificance.

It's clear that Macbeth considers the consequences of his actions. He goes into the act of murder aware of what may come of it. He has also realised, almost immediately, that he has destroyed his own conscience after the murder and he appears to embrace it. Whatever we think of Macbeth for his actions, we can't say that he is naïve or blind to what he is doing. Lady Macbeth, on the other hand, believes that "a little water clears us of this deed", and later says "how easy it is then". To Lady Macbeth, she believes that murder is easy and straightforward. She has no experience of this as her husband does and she hasn't thought things through as her husband has done. In this light, we don't see Shakespeare's portrayal of Lady Macbeth as a strong powerful character but, in fact, as a weak and naïve character who doesn't understand the full import of her actions. She doesn't understand anything until later although there is some acknowledgement of what they've done when she admits that she couldn't carry out the murder herself, saying that if Duncan hadn't reminded her of her own father as he slept "I had done't".

We can see Shakespeare's portrayal of Lady Macbeth in one sense as subverting feminine stereotypes of the Elizabethan and Jacobean eras but also, in a contradictory way, reaffirming them. She doesn't think rationally and logically about the consequences of their actions and, her mad grab for power ends up destroying her and reducing her to a caricature of female helplessness in Act 5. Significantly, we see another parallel between Act 1 Scene 5 and Act 5 Scene 1 when Lady Macbeth goes from encouraging the spirits of darkness to being afraid of the dark. The gentlewoman in Act 5 Scene 1 confirms that Lady Macbeth has light by her all through the night, "tis her command".

Finally, another point that undermines the idea of Shakespeare being a proto-feminist lies in Lady Macbeth's demands to be unsexed by the spirits in Act 1 Scene 5. There is an acknowledgement here that her feminine qualities need to be removed before she can achieve her ambitions, emphasising the idea that women are not naturally equipped with the faculties to be ambitious and achieve their desires. Also, despite the fact that she is technically no longer a 'lady' having been unsexed, she then deploys what we might consider 'feminine tricks' to encourage her husband to murder Duncan. Many productions depict her being seductive and flirtatious, particularly in Act 1 Scene 7, when she eventually convinces Macbeth to carry out the deed.

Was Shakespeare a proto-feminist then? Or was he a traditionalist, simply part of the patriarchal system that subjugated women and treated them as property? Both of these statements are probably too simplistic. Shakespeare was fascinated by complexity and contrast between and within characters in his play and Lady Macbeth is no different. The contradictions, desires, ambitions and fears that she espouses make her a rounded and full character for critics and scholars to disagree about hundreds of years later.

Banquo

The simplest way to look at the character of Banquo is to see him as a foil, a secondary character whose traits and actions serve to highlight something important about the main protagonist. Banquo is Macbeth's friend and someone who is of equal rank to him. They are perfect parallels. They are both present when the Witches deliver their prophecies and, it's often forgotten, Banquo receives a prophecy also, that although he won't be a king, he would "get kings". This means that he will 'beget' kings or, in other words, his descendants would be kings.

Despite the fact that both of these men, of equal position in the social hierarchy, receive prophecies from the "weird sisters", only Macbeth takes matters into his own hands and embarks on his bloody campaign of violence. Banquo's role as a foil here is perfect. He doesn't succumb to the prophecies in the same way as Macbeth because he doesn't have the same hamartia or fatal flaw. He is not ambitious in the way that Macbeth is. Therefore, Banquo could be the perfect embodiment of Shakespeare's warning of selfish individualism.

The character that Banquo is based on, again from Holinshed's Chronicles, reveals some interesting distinctions. In the source material, Banquo was a part of the plot to kill the king along with Macbeth. Shakespeare alters this in his own play to paint Banquo in a good light, possibly because it was believed that King James I was a descendant of Banquo. Remember, Banquo's prophecy was that he would 'beget' kings. Shakespeare's own king, of whom he was a servant, was said to be one of these. In this light, Banquo would simply have to be presented in a sympathetic light.

Shakespeare goes further in his presentation of Banquo as good through his reaction to the witches. Whereas Macbeth believes in the witches at first sight and even echoes their language and their metre, his very first words of the play being "So foul and fair a day I have not seen", Banquo questions their very existence. The witches only speak to Banquo when he insists upon it. Perhaps they recognise in him a resistance to evil that is not present in Macbeth? Similarly, Macbeth requests that the witches stay and speak more to him, Banquo makes it clear that he "neither beg[s] nor fear[s] [their] favours nor [their] fate."

The main distinction then, between Banquo and Macbeth is how they respond to evil. Banquo openly admits that he has thought of their prophecies subsequently and also allows the possibility that if their predictions proved true for Macbeth then he could also hope that his might come true. But there is a huge difference between hoping a prophecy comes true and taking fate into one's own hands as Macbeth did.

There are some reservations, however, about how good Banquo really is. At the beginning, he does remind Macbeth that "sometimes, to win us to their harm, the instruments of darkness tell us…" but shortly after the murder, Banquo remarks that Macbeth "has it all" but fears that he played "most foully for it". This is an acknowledgement that Banquo suspects Macbeth. But why does Banquo not sound the alarm? Why does he not raise objections or even refuse to support the king, like Macduff does? A line in Act 2 Scene 1 gives us a better idea.

Macbeth tells Banquo that should he "cleave to his consent" when the time comes that it may work out well for him. Banquo's response is very vague and he simply says that, so long as he loses no honour by doing so he will. At best, Banquo here is morally ambiguous and at worst he is conspiring with the person he suspects has killed the king.

Another enlightening scene is when Banquo and Fleance are in the castle before the murder of Duncan. Banquo admits to having disturbed sleep while thinking about the witches' prophecies and he asks Fleance to "hold [his] sword" at one stage perhaps hinting that he can't trust himself not to do something evil with it. It also should be remembered that Banquo is silent for forty lines after he learns of Duncan's death. It is almost as if he's paralysed by Macbeth's actions. The appropriate action would be to show loyalty to the rightful heir, Malcolm and stand in support of his claim to the throne but instead he does nothing.

Ultimately, however, Banquo's resistance to evil and his goodness are what cost him his life. Many critics observe that Macbeth, representing evil and Banquo, representing good, can't exist together – only one can survive. Either Macbeth destroys Banquo or is destroyed by him. When Macbeth agonises over this decision he says something very telling about Banquo, he refers to his "wisdom that doth guide his valour". He is acknowledging that the thing he fears most about Banquo is his good and wise nature.

Whether Shakespeare was simply rewriting the history books in order to please King James I or rewriting his source material to tell an even better story, Banquo is a character that is often misunderstood in terms of his complexity. He is good where Macbeth is evil, he leaves things up to chance where Macbeth takes fate into his own hands. The character of Banquo complements Macbeth insofar as it highlights Macbeth's downfall but Banquo himself is no angel. His actions and his indecision in the face of treason paint him out to be a more complex character that we may imagine. Perhaps Shakespeare is allowing for the fact that nobody is perfect, no person is all good or all evil but the conflict within Macbeth that leads him to evil deeds appears to have the opposite result in Banquo, yet more evidence of Shakespeare's fascination with complex characters, contrasts and opposites.

The witches

The presence of the three witches in *Macbeth* is one of the most talked about elements of the play. Their importance is immediately clear as they are the very first thing that the audience sees, appearing on stage in Act one Scene one to set the tone for the rest of the play. While it is undeniable that belief in witches in Shakespeare's time was relatively common, it wasn't necessarily widespread and there would have been large amounts of scepticism form some members of the audience about what they were watching.

One of the most common reasons given for Shakespeare's inclusion of the witches in his play is in order to please the new king, King James I. King James I was very much interested in witchcraft and even published a book on the subject in 1597 called *Daemonologie*. He had a great desire to spread knowledge and fear of witches and witchcraft – something that was more popular in Scotland that in England by the time King James I came to the English throne – and some of it seems to come from personal experience.

In 1589, King James was due to marry Queen Anne of Denmark. On her voyage across the North Sea to meet her new husband, Queen Anne's ship was hit by severe storms that nearly cost her her life. Prevented from sailing further, she returned to Denmark. James decided to sail to Denmark himself to collect her in person and, on their return voyage to Scotland, their ships were once again, hit by severe storms that almost claimed both their lives. James was convinced it was the result of witchcraft and, upon returning to Scotland, he had no fewer than 70 'witches' from the coastal town of North Berwick rounded up, interrogated and tortured until many of them 'confessed' that they were witches and they had been responsible for the storms and they were executed.

King James had all of this published in a pamphlet with the gory details included so that he could spread fear of witches around Scotland and beyond. It is of little surprise then that *Macbeth*, set in Scotland, uses witches both to inspire a sense of curiosity and potentially fear in the audience as well as play up to the King's interests in the subject.

There are also some other interpretations of the witches however that are interesting in the context of the rest of the play. Witches in the Elizabethan and Jacobean eras were, by and large, old women. Banquo, upon first seeing the witches In Act 1 Scene 3, says that their "beards forbids" him from believing that they are female. They are similarly described throughout the play as "hags" or "withered and wild". One of the other descriptions is, however, "weird sisters". While the stage directions refer to them as witches, within the play itself, they are most often referred to as the "weird sisters" or "weird women" and actually, only once as witches in the dialogue.

The meaning of 'weird' here isn't similar to the way we would use the word to describe something strange or peculiar but instead, the word refers to the idea of destiny. So then, the weird sisters could in fact be the goddesses of destiny, associated with the three classical Fates from Greek mythology, implying that they can, in some way, control destiny or fate. In this light, the witches take on a different role. Rather than simply being there to impress King James I, they may have a more complex function in furthering Shakespeare's exploration of the idea of free-will.

They are clearly evil but their influence and reach is felt far and wide throughout the play. They are more than simply agents of darkness to set the tone but rather, their presence 'infects' the rest of the play as even the characters begin to take on their speech patterns and mimic their word choices. The witches talk of a battle "lost and won" in Act 1 Scene 1 is heard again when Duncan is speaking in the following scene and says "what he hath lost [referring to Cawdor], noble Macbeth hath won". The Witches' couplet "fair is foul and foul is fair", is echoed closely by Macbeth in his very first words in Act 3 Scene 1, "So foul and fair a day I have not seen". We even see this focus on oppositions in Macbeth's first extended soliloquy in Act 1 Scene 3 when he says "This supernatural soliciting cannot be ill, cannot be good... nothing is but what it's not".

Later in the play, the repetition, opposition (which we can also call antithesis) and the Witches' rhyming couplets are heard in Lady Macbeth's own words in Act 3 Scene 2 when she says, "Nought's had, all's spent, where our desire is got without content: 'tis safer to be that which we destroy, than by destruction dwell in doubtful joy".

There are some interpretations of *Macbeth* that suggest that Lady Macbeth is perhaps a fourth witch. There are indeed some things that suggest that this may be the case. In Act 1 Scene 5, Lady Macbeth calls on the powers of darkness to take her over, "to make thick my blood and stop up th' access and passage to remorse". One belief about witches at this time was that their blood was thick and slow moving. This in turn supposedly made their skin hard, like armour, that made them difficult to kill. By calling on the spirits to do something similar with her own blood, Lady Macbeth can be seen to be one of the witches or at least aligned with evil.

Despite all of this however, we also have to question what it is that Shakespeare was trying to show us through the Witches. We can say that they are there to appeal to King James I and we can also say that their influence is felt throughout the play and has a knock-on effect on many different characters but one of the central questions that still gets asked today is this: who's to blame? Would Macbeth have done what he did if he had never met the witches?

If we consider Shakespeare's use of the word "weird" to mean fateful or controlling destiny, then we could look at the witches as agents of destiny and, in that case, perhaps Macbeth was destined to follow this path, to become a tragic figure. There is also, however, a suggestion that the witches' power is limited. In a reference to King James' own personal experience in Act 1 Scene 3, the line "and though his bark cannot be lost/ yet it shall be tempest tossed" tells us that the witches have power over certain things but not over life and death and, as such, they are only suggesting these things to Macbeth and that it is Macbeth himself who is personally responsible for his actions.

Macduff

One way of understanding the character of Macduff is, similarly to Banquo, as a foil for Macbeth. If we consider that Macbeth turns his back, through selfish greed, on the established system and traditions of his country by killing the King and claiming the crown for himself, then Macduff does the complete opposite. He sacrifices everything he has – his wife, his children, his castle – to restore the rightful heir to throne and restore the balance and equilibrium in his country. Through Macduff, the audience sees the correct choices and actions that should be taken by a good subject.

If we recall that Shakespeare was a supporter of royal power and the existing system, it's clear then that Macduff, who is the most outspoken in terms of his desire for revenge, is to be seen as a sort of hero himself. He sacrifices his family not to become king himself, but simply to restore the correct authority in his country. He is a pure traditionalist and as close to the perfect nobleman as you could get.

When Macduff travels to England in Act 4 Scene 3 to meet with Malcolm to get his support to remove Macbeth from the throne, he reveals his deep concern about his country and the way it's going. Speaking to Malcolm, he says "Bleed, bleed, poor country", and later he says "O Scotland, Scotland!". It is clear that Macduff's loyalties lie with his nation, just as Macbeth's seemed to at the beginning of the play, before selfish ambition took over. Macduff, too, isn't willing to sacrifice his country simply to give Malcolm the throne either. When Malcolm, in an effort to test Macduff, lists all of his 'vices', Macduff is willing to overlook his desire for women and riches but when Malcolm says that if he had power he would "pour the sweet milk of concord into hell" and "confound all unity on earth", Macduff says that not only is Malcolm not "fit to govern" he's "not fit to live".

In this scene Shakespeare presents the audience with the ideal version of the royal subject. He is willing to sacrifice all that he has to maintain the system but, ultimately, loyalty to his nation is the number one priority. Macduff's dedication and commitment to his country and his 'real' king makes Macbeth's disregard of it stand out all the more.

When Macbeth and Lady Macbeth carry out their deeds, they repeatedly call on heaven to look away or for light to be put out so they can't be seen. It's an acknowledgement that what they are doing is wrong. There can be few things worse than regicide. When Macduff is informed in Act 4 Scene 3 that his family have been murdered by "the tyrant", he swears revenge. Interestingly, he invokes heaven and brings the idea of God and heaven into his quest. He says, "… gentle heavens,/ cut short all intermission; front to front/Bring thou this fiend of Scotland and myself;/Within my sword's length set him; if he 'scape/Heaven forgive him too!".

Here, Macduff is secure in the knowledge that his desire for revenge is righteous. He asks "gentle heaven" to bring Macbeth before his sword so he can deal with him. Malcolm too invokes heaven when he responds to Macduff telling him "Macbeth is ripe for the shaking, and the powers above put on their instruments". The suggestion here is that they are righteous and that theirs is somehow a holy war against the tyrant Macbeth. Macduff and Malcolm are on the side of God and heaven. All of this confirms the idea that Macduff is an idealised version of the royal subject, deployed to expose and highlight Macbeth's worst excesses.

It's no coincidence that, at the end of the play, it is Macduff who kills Macbeth. If Macduff is the perfect subject and Macbeth is to be viewed as an example of where selfish ambition, then Shakespeare makes a very obvious claim for tradition and upholding the system through the last interaction between the two in Act 5 Scene 8.

Macbeth at first is reluctant to fight Macduff because he feels that his "soul is too much charged" with Macduff family blood already – a reference to the slaughter of Macduff's family. But Macduff, following the lead of Lady Macbeth, calls him a "coward" in order to bait him into doing something he said he didn't want to do and it works. Macbeth, in his final few lines says, "I will not yield/To kiss the ground before young Malcolm's feet" as a good subject would be happy to do.

Macduff re-enters in the next scene carrying Macbeth's head and announces that now "the time is free" and hails Malcolm as "King of Scotland". Shakespeare does something quite interesting here. The fact is that, despite Macbeth's actions, he was the crowned King, and, as such, Macduff has committed regicide, the same crime as Macbeth. But the audience and Macduff himself are protected from this by Macbeth's extreme actions in murdering Macduff's entire family.

It is clear then that Macbeth and Macduff are broadly similar. They are both noble lords, they both have outspoken wives and they both take fate into their own hands – Macbeth to claim the crown and Macduff, travelling to England to restore the rightful heir. Macbeth's actions are all prompted by selfishness, greed and personal ambition whereas Macduff's actions are prompted by his love for his country and the rightful king. Macduff then shows up Macbeth to be lacking in loyalty and traditional values.

The Porter

Act 2 Scene 3, also known as The Porter's scene, is a curious one in *Macbeth*. Some scholars and critics have dismissed it as almost "un-Shakespearean" and, therefore irrelevant. Others have identified the scene as simple 'comic relief' after the murder of King Duncan in the previous scene, a contrast between the horrors carried out by Macbeth and the crude humour of the Porter. The most common consensus, however, is that this scene and the Porter himself, is vitally important to the rest of the play and does much more than get a few laughs from the audience.

In summary, the porter is a servant of the Macbeth household whose job it is to answer to callers to the castle gates. The porter has been up late, enjoying the celebrations with King Duncan and the other guests and, so, he is tired but also, hungover having drank too much. When he hears the knocking, that of Macduff who has come to wake the king, he imagines that the knocking is that at the gate of hell and he is the porter for hell's gate.

He imagines himself admitting three different sinners into Hell. The first is a farmer who tried to make money by hoarding his grain in the hope that the price would rise but, when the price drops, he realises he's financially ruined and hangs himself. The second is the equivocator (there's a link here with the witches and their equivocation) who has committed treason but tries to get himself out of it by telling half-truths. The third is an English tailor who has been condemned for stealing by making clothes with less material than he charges for. All three of these sinners are condemned to death and the porter imagines welcoming them to hell.

In defence of those who argue that the scene is all about providing comic relief after the intensity of Duncan's murder, the humour comes from the fact that these were all topical events at the time that *Macbeth* would have been first performed. The farmer who hangs himself on the "expectation of plenty" would have been despised by many as someone looking to profit on the regular food shortages of Shakespeare's era. Interestingly. Shakespeare himself was fined for hoarding grain in times of shortages while waiting for the best price. The equivocator is widely believed to refer to Father Garnet, a Jesuit priest who was hanged for his role in the Gunpowder Plot – the catholic plot to kill King James I shortly before *Macbeth* was written. Finally, the English tailor and the French hose refers to the changing fashions of the time where French hose became so tight-fitting that any skimping of material would have been noticed immediately. Therefore, the English tailor who had been cheating his customers for years, finally gets found out when the fashion changes.

The audience would have understood these references and they are certain to have generated some laughs, especially when they are taken with the Porter's later conversation with Macduff about drinking and sexual performance, but we can also look at the function of the porter and his scene in three other ways.

Firstly, Shakespeare could be normalising Macbeth's crimes in the previous scene. By putting his actions alongside 'ordinary' crimes such as stealing and greed and lying, his actions don't seem big in scale, they seem lowly and cowardly – murdering an old man as he slept in his bed. Macbeth has become no different to an ordinary low criminal through his actions. It serves the function of lowering the standard against which Macbeth's crimes are to be judged. As the famous critic John B. Harcourt puts it, "this process continues through the association of Macbeth with a petty speculator, with a known traitor... and with a tailor." Macbeth's murder is an ugly deed when put alongside these smaller crimes.

So perhaps, by listing these 'smaller' crimes that condemn their culprits to hell, immediately after the murder of Duncan, Shakespeare is trying to emphasise that Macbeth's actions are not other-worldly or noble or outside of the realm on consequences. They are lowly and common and ugly. But, alternatively, Shakespeare could also be emphasising the monstrous nature of Macbeth and how he is, in fact, closer to real evil than these other criminals.

The Porter speaks to Macduff about alcohol and what it does to a man. He talks at length about sexual performance, how alcohol encourages a man to want sex but stops him from being able to perform. In Act 2 Scene 3 he says, "It sets him on, and it takes him off; it persuades him, and disheartens him; makes him stand to, and not stand to; in conclusion, equivocates him". It's clear that, for the porter, alcohol and sexual desire are vices that he battles with. He refers to being under the influence of alcohol almost like demonic possession. There is no question that Macbeth does not share these vices. There are no references to Macbeth indulging in alcohol or women.

Shakespeare, here, could be suggesting that the 'simple' vices of the Porter – alcohol, women – are not as bad as Macbeth's vices – greed, self-seeking ambition and pride. Macduff himself, when he meets with Malcolm, echoes this when he suggests that Malcolm's vices wouldn't prevent him from being king until he says that he wants to destroy peace. According to Harcourt, "The simple vices of the porter establish an ethical distance between the failings of ordinary humanity and the monstrous evil now within the castle walls."

The third way of examining this scene is one that Shakespeare is echoing his message about free-will, fate and the sanctity of the state. When we examine the crimes of the three imaginary sinners, we see that they roughly correlate with Macbeth's own actions. The farmer's sin is self-seeking greed, the equivocator's crime is treason and the tailor's crime is theft of clothing that properly belongs to others (see here all the references to clothing in the play). Macbeth is guilty of all of these sins also and, in each of these cases, the sinners' own actions led to their deaths. It is only logical that Macbeth's actions will also lead to his death.

On a final note, there is something hopeful in the Porter's speech. It doesn't appear so from the outset but in all his descriptions of his 'battle' with alcohol where he describes a physical fight – "being too strong for him, though he took up my legs sometime…". This battle of an individual man against alcohol is won ultimately by the man when he vomits the alcohol up "I made a shift to cast him". Similarly, the evil in the state of Scotland will also be purged or removed – the killing of Macbeth by Duncan. The Porter, in many ways, is a representative of ordinary people and he is looking to the future.

Scene by Scene Analysis

Shakespeare's Macbeth was written sometime around 1605-1606. The first recorded performance was in 1606 and it is widely seen as one of the most powerful and dark plays in Shakespeare's collection. The play is loosely based on real events. There was a history book in Shakespeare's day called Holinshed's Chronicles, with which many people would have been familiar and in it there was the story of King Macbeth of Scotland, Macduff and Duncan. The play itself differs greatly from the real-life Macbeth but there may be a hint in the Gaelic nickname he had, Ri Deircc, which translates as "the red king".

It is one of Shakespeare's most famous plays and tells the story of a Scottish general who receives a prophecy from three witches that one day he will become King of Scotland. Unable to control his ambitions and encouraged by his wife, he kills the King and takes the throne for himself. After this, however, he is forced to commit further murders to stay on the throne and the guilt and psychological damage that come with his decisions eventually topple both him and his wife.

Another interesting sub-plot to this play is that Shakespeare's King, King James, was supposed to have been a descendant of Banquo, one of the central characters in the play. Considering King James was Shakespeare's benefactor, he would have had to make sure that Banquo was presented in a good light and there is a suggestion in Holinshed's Chronicles that Banquo was much more of a villain in real life.

The play has a wealth of moral dilemmas and themes for students to explore. Also, it is rich in structural and language techniques that students will explore through the analysis of each scene. In order to highlight key techniques, themes and ideas they will be presented in bold in the analysis.

Shakespeare makes use of **dramatic irony**, often presenting the audience with situations where we know more about what is going on than the characters do. This enhances both the tension in the play and also the audience's involvement. There is also a lot to be said about the **language** Shakespeare employs throughout the play. As you will see in the first part of analysis, Shakespeare uses **iambic pentameter** to distinguish between different *types* of characters. In many parts of the play, language also reflects the state-of-mind of characters, mainly Macbeth.

Language is also used in a devious way and links to one of the main **themes** in the play, the idea of **appearance versus reality**. In many of the key scenes of the play, there are half-truths being told, characters hiding behind masks (metaphorically speaking) and pretending to be one thing while doing another.

Many of the **metaphors** we see surround being one thing while doing or saying or meaning something different. We also see metaphors dealing with clothing – putting on or taking off different garments meaning or suggesting that the character is putting on different personalities or pretending to be different people.

As with many of Shakespeare's plays, there is also a strong link to **nature**. Many of the language techniques he uses for comparison invoke natural imagery. When he is talking about the witches, Shakespeare uses base or lower creatures such as toads, rats and snakes. There is also a very interesting parallel that Shakespeare sets up between nature and the play. Often, we see the effects of what men do in the play carried out in nature. So, for example, if a man kills a king, then we see something equally 'unnatural' in nature – a small bird killing a hawk, a horse kicking against his master.

This **natural order** also relates to why this play is seen as one of Shakespeare's **tragedies**. For his play to be a tragedy, the main protagonist or central character must fall from a high position (socially) because of some tragic flaw (hamartia) within themselves. In *Macbeth*, the main protagonist decides to kill the king to fulfil his ambitions and this leads to his downfall. According to the strict hierarchy in Shakespeare's time, the king was at the top and no one from below him (lords, noblemen, soldiers or peasants) could move up. This is what Macbeth does and in order to put the social order back to normal, he must be removed (killed) and the rightful heir must take the throne.

This opens up some of the **key questions** in the play. Academics have long argued some of the finer points of this play and some of the issues that arise time and again are questions about motive. Would Macbeth have killed his king without the presence of female characters in the play (Lady Macbeth and the witches)? Is Shakespeare making a comment on the power or influence of women? Is Macbeth's fatal flaw ambition or greed? Or is Macbeth simply a weak man who gives in to the desires of others and allows himself to be caught up in their wishes and plans?

Structure is another key element to this play and, throughout, Shakespeare makes use of things like **foreshadowing** and **echoing**. Often, ideas or imagery are used at one point in the play to signal a later development. At the beginning, for example, the Thane of Cawdor is executed for being a traitor. His title, *Cawdor*, is given to Macbeth – who also turns out to be a traitor.

These links strengthen the narrative of the play and can also act like signposts for the reader/audience to follow on their journey through the story. They are also useful for students to demonstrate their knowledge of the play. When speaking about a significant part, it can be related to a later event displaying both textual knowledge and awareness of structural techniques.

Finally, one of the overriding questions that persists throughout the play is whether or not the audience can have sympathy for Macbeth. For it to be a tragedy, we must feel some sympathy for him at the end, otherwise it's just a story of a very bad person who gets what he deserves. Shakespeare, as you will see through the analysis of each scene, works very hard on the **structure** and the **language** to present Macbeth as a character for whom we can feel sympathy. By shielding him from some of the most horrific moments and using language to expose his despair and isolation, Shakespeare is trying to present a multi-faceted character who, despite his actions, holds onto the reader's emotions and sympathy until the very end.

Whether or not he succeeds is, of course, entirely up to you.

Act 1 Scene 1

This is one of the most famous scenes in *Macbeth*. It is the first time the audience gets to see the witches and we are invited into a mysterious world inhabited by creatures which, as of yet, we are unsure are for good or evil. Shakespeare uses the witches as a way of pulling in the audience. We arrive at the end of whatever it is they have been doing. The first line we hear is "*When shall we three meet again*".

In Elizabethan times, the witches would have been a big draw for audiences because there was a huge amount of interest (and belief) in witchcraft and the supernatural.

Their meeting is complete and whatever they were up to, we can only guess. Shakespeare is clever in his construction here, prompting our curiosity about what role the witches will play in the play. It also helps to set the scene for the rest of the play. This is a dark world where there's confusion and not everything is what it seems. The scene opens with thunder and lightning, it continues with the witches taking about "*hurly-burly*" and when a battle is both "*lost and won*".

This sense of things being not what they seem, of appearance versus reality, is very important for the rest of the play as we see that many of the most important moments are based on this contrast.

The scene closes and we, as the audience, are none the wiser about what is happening. The last lines *"Fair is foul and foul is fair/hover through the fog and the filthy air"* seem to reinforce the idea that this is a frightening, mysterious world where the supernatural holds some power. The fact that Shakespeare structures the play so as to show this to the audience first is quite significant.

A note about **form** and **structure**:

You will notice that when the witches speak in scene 1, they speak in rhyme. This rhyme scheme is known as rhyming couplets. Shakespeare used the language in his plays to signify the importance or rank of the person speaking.

For example, all of the nobles in *Macbeth* speak in **Iambic Pentameter**. This is where you have **five stressed and five unstressed syllables**.

For example:

> *"And fixed his head upon our battlements"*

This line contains **five iambs** (a pair of syllables with one stressed and the other unstressed).

So:

> *"And fixed his head upon our battlements"*

This gives an even and almost 'sing-song' quality to the lines. If you replace the actual words from the above example it simply sounds like:

"Da-**dum** da-**dum**, da-**dum**. da-**dum**, da-**dum**"

This is known as **Blank Verse**. A lot of Shakespeare's writing is done this way – it simply means the words don't have to rhyme but it must be written in iambic pentameter.

This is important because certain characters, such as the witches, don't use iambic pentameter and it's a good point to be able to make, to distinguish between the form used for different characters and different types of character.

The witches use of rhyming couplets give a sinister air to the play. It's like a nursery rhyme but much darker and evil. It's difficult to appreciate the effect of these witches now in the 21st century. To us the rhyming and spells can often come across as silly and humorous but this would not have been the case for Shakespeare's audiences.

The form used by the witches is **Trochaic Tetrameter**. Again, this is quite easy to understand once you break it down. A **Trochee** is the opposite of an **Iamb**. Whereas the iamb contains two syllables with the first one unstressed and the second stressed (*"and **fixed**"*) a trochee is the other way around, a stressed followed by unstressed.

For example:

"Fair is foul and foul is fair"

In this line from the witches you stress the words as follows:

"Fair** is **foul** and **foul** is **fair"

The word tetrameter just means there are four pairs of these trochees. The trochaic tetrameter added to the rhyming couplets makes for an entertaining scene and a clear break, on Shakespeare's part, between the witches and the other characters in the play.

Act 1 Scene 2

Again, like scene 1, this scene gives us important information to help us understand the rest of the play. The main part of this scene is the wounded sergeant who has come from the battle to tell Duncan (and also the audience) about what has happened.

Macbeth and, to a lesser extent, Banquo are described through their actions in battle and this is the first we hear about these characters. In this respect, Shakespeare is presenting the character of Macbeth to us through the opinions of other people.

This has two effects. The first is to build anticipation in the audience for when they do meet Macbeth – after all, the play is named after him, he has to be a big deal! The second effect is to show the audience how well-respected Macbeth is by the other characters in the play – the other noblemen in Scotland. This gives the subsequent events in the play much more drama and emotional impact. He is universally loved at the beginning of the play and, through his own actions, he ruins everything he has.

The "bloody" sergeant describes Macbeth as "brave" and that "he deserves that name". He goes on to tell Duncan about how Macbeth was so skilled in battle that his sword didn't even have time to cool down from all the blood that he was spilling and that it "smok'd with bloody execution".
All of the imagery that the sergeant uses in this scene is brutal, blood-filled and shocking. He finishes the first part of his re-telling by describing how Macbeth "carved" a path through the soldiers of the rebel forces and found the rebel leader, Macdonwald who he "unseam'd" from his nave to his chaps".

The response to this is not one of horror. The idea of Macbeth literally unzipping a man from his belly to his chin, chopping his head off and putting it on a stake is, to the King and his men, admirable and praise-worthy.

This gives us a good indication of the sort of world in which the play is set. It's very masculine, violent and honour-bound. In order to be considered a good and worthy man, you have to prove yourself in battle and one who kills people in large numbers in battle is certainly thought of as good. Later in this scene we learn that a Scottish nobleman, the Thane of Cawdor, betrayed Scotland and sided with the King of Norway in an attempt to invade.

He is stripped of his title, which is then given to Macbeth as a reward for his bravery and loyalty, "What he hath lost, noble Macbeth hath won". Here Shakespeare is creating an interesting paradox. While we are supposed to see the contrast between a disloyal, treasonous Thane (Cawdor) and a loyal brave one (Macbeth), by the end of the play they are very similar with Macbeth going on to betray his king and his country. This is an example of **foreshadowing** or echoing, a technique Shakespeare uses throughout the play.

One of the last lines of this scene reinforces how brutal this world is and how low a value is put on life. Duncan orders Cawdor's death in five words with no show or ceremony, "Go, pronounce his present death". It's done in a matter of seconds with no sentimentality or enquiry.

Act 1 Scene 3

Here we return to the witches. The first scene is given over entirely to the witches and the second to human beings. In the third we have the two together. The language Shakespeare uses when the witches are speaking is always rude, vulgar and shocking. Animals are also referred to frequently which can be seen as symbolising the witches' links to nature and lower-level animals. The animals in scene 1, the cat and the toad, were considered witches' familiars or pets. The animal imagery is used quite a lot throughout the play in a number of different contexts.

We see Macbeth from time to time slip into the way of speech associated with the witches, which could be interpreted as Shakespeare's way of showing us the impact the witches and assorted 'dark spirits' are having on him.

In this scene we are being shown the 'power' of the witches. It's not as great, however, as we are led to believe in scene 1. For example, the audience finds out that one of the witches has been away "killing swine" while the first witch has been offended by some woman who wouldn't give her chestnuts. These events don't exactly inspire true fear in the audience. The witch who has been offended by the woman with the chestnuts has decided to take it out on the woman's husband who is a sailor. She has control over the winds and uses them to disrupt the ship's journey. It's important to remember, however, that she does not have the power to take his life "Though his bark cannot be lost, / yet it shall be tempest-tost".

Shakespeare makes great us of foreshadowing and hinting at things to come as structural devices in *Macbeth* and many of his other plays and there are some good examples in this passage about the sailor. At the outset, the witch says "I'll drain him dry as hay" which can be read as a comment on Macbeth and his fate as he is ultimately drained morally, physically and spiritually by the end of the play. Another important piece of foreshadowing is when the witch says that one of the ways she will torture this sailor is by preventing him from sleeping.

"Sleep shall neither night nor day, / hang upon his penthouse lid." Sleep is natural and important for people to stay physically strong but also mentally. It is a natural process but Macbeth, through his unnatural deeds, removes sleep as an option for himself.

This scene is also important for developing the characters of Macbeth and Banquo and especially the differences between them. Shakespeare is using Banquo as a contrast to Macbeth to show the audience that what Macbeth does and the tragedy that befalls him is as much his own fault as anyone else's.

Banquo's response to the witches is that he's simply not very interested in what they have to say and he is also a little sceptical and wary. He tells them that he "neither beg[s] nor fear[s] your favours nor your hate" and asks them for a prophecy. Banquo is also surprised by Macbeth's reaction to the witches telling him he will be king. He asks Macbeth "Why do you start, and seem to fear things that do sound so fair?"

There is a structural point here. Shakespeare intends for his audience to believe that this isn't the first time thoughts of becoming king have entered his head. We can read into this some of Macbeth's guilt. He has clearly thought about this before. Otherwise, why would he react to such good news with fear rather than surprise? Also, the thoughts he has afterwards about murder are surely the thoughts of a person who has previously thought about the murder of Duncan: "whose horrid image doth unfix my hair, / and make my seated heart knock at my ribs".

It's also interesting to note that Macbeth wants to know more from the witches and also wants to know from where they get their "strange intelligence". Whereas Banquo simply regards their prophecies as "honest trifles". Unimportant things could, however, cause men to do terrible things because of temptation. Little does he know how right he will be.

Macbeth's first words in this scene are also his first in the play and it is telling that they are so in tune with the witches from the opening scene. Macbeth says "So foul and fair a day I have not seen". It could be suggested that Shakespeare is linking him with the supernatural and evil element of the play from his very first appearance.

Act 1 Scene 4

Dramatic irony is a device that Shakespeare uses to increase the drama and tension in his plays. Dramatic irony is where a character is unaware of a crucial bit of information of which the audience is aware. This way, we watch the character make decisions without the full picture and it gives the audience a sense of being involved in the play. We desperately want to share the knowledge that we have, but obviously cannot.

In this scene Shakespeare makes use of dramatic irony in quite an important way. We are told that the Thane of Cawdor, who had turned traitor, has been executed. But we are also told about how he died which, in this honour-bound, masculine society, is very important. He died a good death according to Malcolm which is in contrast to how Macbeth takes on the title of Cawdor.

The audience already knows that Macbeth is considering killing Duncan to take the throne from the previous scene. So, in that sense, everything here is dramatic irony. Macbeth takes on the title of someone who was a traitor and he himself has betrayal of the worst kind on his mind. Duncan talks about how difficult it is to know what someone is thinking when they are keeping it hidden. He says it's difficult to "find the mind's construction in the face". He also goes on to tell us that "he was a man in whom I built an absolute trust" and we know that another man whom he trusts completely, his "peerless kinsman" Macbeth, is also plotting something which he wants to keep hidden.

In this scene the audience is being shown how Macbeth's journey into deception, evil and brutality is beginning even now, not long after the witches made their prophecies. Duncan heaps praise on Macbeth for his part in the battle, almost to the point of embarrassing himself: "My plenteous joys, / Wanton in fullness, seek to hide themselves / in drops of sorrow". He's saying that he's so happy that he could cry. Whereas Macbeth responds in short, basic language which shows the audience that Macbeth is not on the same wave-length as Duncan, he can't be as happy as him because of the thoughts in his mind.

Shakespeare does this often throughout the play. He uses the language that his characters speak to point out differences. The hyperbolic, overblown language of Duncan shows the audience that he is completely unaware of what is going on behind the scenes and Shakespeare uses this to create a sense of anticipation in his audience. We are watching Duncan heap lavish praise on the man who is going to kill him.

Macbeth gives a speech about how loyal he is, how doing service and protecting the king is in itself a reward: "The service and loyalty I owe, / In doing it, pays itself." Macbeth here, is doing exactly what the previous Thane of Cawdor did, hiding his real thoughts in false words. This shows us that

Macbeth has decided that he is going to be treacherous and hide his true feelings from everyone around – one of the key themes in the entire play.

This scene also has one of the most crucial elements in the play. In Scotland at this time, the King was allowed to name his successor and that person didn't necessarily have to be in his family. This was to prevent any fighting and disputes between noblemen in the event that the king died suddenly. Duncan names his son, Malcolm, as his successor (the successor to the King is named the Prince of Cumberland). This effectively seals Duncan's fate as Macbeth now believes he has no choice but to kill Duncan to be king. Once he hears this news, Macbeth barely gives a response before riding off to his castle to help his wife "prepare" for the king and the noblemen who are coming to stay that evening.

Macbeth's line to himself immediately before he leaves the rest of the noblemen and the king is quite telling. He says: "The Prince of Cumberland, that is a step on which I must fall down or else o'er leap, for in my way it lies. Stars, hide your fires! Let not light see my black and deep desires." Here he is admitting that he will need to do something terrible to become king. He sees Malcolm being named as successor as something he must overcome. This focuses his mind on what needs to be done and he asks the stars to not shine light on his plans.

This will become a very important theme throughout the rest of the play – appearance versus reality, things being hidden from sight, what is versus what's not.

Act 1 Scene 5

Behind every great man, it is said, there is a great woman. This scene is the first glimpse the audience gets of the woman who knows Macbeth better than any other. Better, it almost seems, than he knows himself. Up until this point, we are shown Macbeth the soldier, the warrior, the public face of the great thane. In this scene we are introduced to the private side of Macbeth, the one that remains hidden from the other thanes and noblemen of Scotland.

Lady Macbeth is very clear on what needs to happen. She openly admits that, despite her husband's ambition, he is incapable of acting dishonourably to get what he wants. She fears his "nature" and believes him to have too much "human kindness". Lady Macbeth's "fear" in this case is not fear of her husband or what he might do - it is the fear that he is incapable of killing Duncan: an act that would make her Queen.

The theme of **appearance versus reality** or confusion and opposites re-emerges here. Lady Macbeth says that Macbeth is honourable and kind. To her, just as to the witches, this is a bad thing. The witches say: "Fair is foul and foul is fair" while Lady Macbeth scorns her husband's good qualities because she knows that they will not make him king. The rest of this scene involves Lady Macbeth invoking evil spirits to help her to achieve her goals.

This needs to be understood in the context it was intended. For Shakespeare's audience, dedicating oneself to evil and calling on demonic spirits would have been very powerful. Lady Macbeth is crossing over to the dark side here and there is evidence to suggest that she has, in fact, become possessed. Later in the play we see her sleepwalking, unable to sleep properly and talking to herself. These are all symptoms Shakespeare's audience would have understood as being possessed by demons.

Shakespeare also uses an interesting metaphor to extend the idea of things not being as they are. Towards the end of the scene, Lady Macbeth has decided that Duncan is to be murdered and she proceeds to give her husband a lesson on hiding his true feelings and thoughts. She tells him that he is giving the game away simply by his face: "Your face, my thane, is as a book where men may read strange matters." She advises him to "look like the innocent flower, but be the serpent under't". Here we have the metaphor of concealment, confusion and hidden identity and also it is another allusion to the animal imagery that Shakespeare employs earlier in the play.

Finally, I think it's interesting to note Macbeth's response here. His wife has told him, in no uncertain terms, that Duncan is to be murdered and all he says in response is: "We will speak further". Is this a man who has already decided what he is going to do or is he simply trying to fob his wife off, to not start an argument with her? Shakespeare is beginning to add extra dimensions and characteristics to Macbeth. We have now seen Macbeth the warrior, Macbeth the worrier and Macbeth the private man. His relationship with his wife is interesting because it shows us who is in charge. It's almost as if all the noblemen and other characters in the play fear and respect Macbeth, while his wife looks down on him slightly. This has important consequences for his character.

Act 1 Scene 6

The calm before the storm. Here we see Duncan arrive at Macbeth's castle completely unaware of the plotting and scheming going on inside. It is this irony that makes the scene appealing to the reader. Duncan speaks very generously about the castle while Lady Macbeth plays the willing hostess. Duncan says that the "castle hath a pleasant seat; the air nimbly and sweetly recommends itself unto our gentle senses". While praising the beauty of where he is to be murdered, he also speaks very warmly to Lady Macbeth.

It is clear that Duncan has the utmost respect and love for both Macbeth and Lady Macbeth and this scene is here because it is building up the shock the audience will feel at the king's death. He feels as safe as he possibly could in this place and Lady Macbeth is incredibly skilled at looking like the flower but being the serpent under it. The final image of this short scene is the "honoured hostess" leading the king by the hand to his own grave.

Another element of **dramatic irony** here in this scene is Duncan's presumption that Macbeth rode ahead at speed in order to prepare for his king's visit. In one sense he did, but it was to prepare for his murder and not his reception.

Act 1 Scene 7

A **soliloquy** is a piece in a play where a character speaks as if to him or herself. There may be others present on stage or nearby but we are supposed to take it that they are unable to hear what is being said. In this scene, we have one of Macbeth's most important soliloquies. Essentially, Macbeth puts forward an incredibly logical and convincing argument as to why he shouldn't kill his king. He considers the fate of a murderer and admits that, once you've killed one person, it's often a slippery slope. His opening lines of the soliloquy tell us this. He says: "If it were done when 'tis done, then 'twere well it were done quickly."

This can be interpreted in two ways. Firstly, if the murder has to be done then it should be done fast to get it over and done with. This would show a reluctance on Macbeth's part. He simply wants to get this terrible deed over and done with and shows no blood lust. However, the next lines seem to suggest that this actually means if it were done and finished. An **alternative interpretation** would be to read these lines as: "If it's all done and finished with the murder of Duncan then I'd do it as soon as possible". Here he is worried about what comes after the murder. He admits that these deeds often cause knock-on effects and he is worried that the murder of Duncan will create a chain of events out of his control.

Shakespeare uses the technique of **foreshadowing** here as in other parts of the play because Macbeth is completely correct. His murder of Duncan ultimately brings about his own downfall. Macbeth's argument *against* the murder is so compelling in this scene. He says that he shouldn't kill him because he is his king, he's also his relative and he's a guest in his home as well. He goes on the say that Duncan has been a great King and is loved and respected by all; killing him would cause a terrible reaction from the people of Scotland. He even goes so far as to say that he has no good reason to kill Duncan, "no spur", except his ambition.

At this point in his speech, however, Lady Macbeth enters. This is an interesting structural technique from Shakespeare as it gives the audience a visual cue. Macbeth has "no spur", no cause to murder his king except his ambition and, now, here enters Lady Macbeth. The fact that she arrived just at the point where he has made such a clear and logical argument *against* the murder is significant.

One of the key questions in the whole play is whether or not Lady Macbeth is to blame for the events which take place and this scene is often used as evidence in arguments about it. Macbeth decides that "we will proceed no further in this business" and Lady Macbeth destroys his resolve and all his convincing arguments in less than fifty lines of dialogue. Remember, this is Macbeth the warrior, the fearless leader in battle and he is verbally battered and destroyed by his wife.

She tackles him using a number of different techniques. Firstly, she says that he is inconsistent and changes his mind often ("Was the hope drunk, wherin you dressed yourself? Hath it slept since"). Secondly she uses his love for her against him saying that he obviously doesn't love her if he won't do this ("From this time such I account thy love"). Thirdly, he is no better than someone who is drunk all the time, deciding things when they are hung over and then changing their mind ("And wakes it now, to look so green and pale"). Finally, and most importantly, she challenges his manhood ("When you durst do it, then you were a man").

This is the most effective attack because Macbeth's entire reputation is founded upon his bravery and courage and she is basically calling him the Shakespearean equivalent of 'chicken'. She calls him "coward", "poor cat" and says "then you were a man" until he gives in. He has no answer to these attacks and the entire play hinges on four little words he then utters: "If we should fail?"

This isn't Macbeth arguing against the murder; he's already given in to his wife. This is Macbeth looking for her to take the reins, to tell him what the plan is so he can follow her rather than decide anything for himself. He is completely under her 'spell' (similar to the witches) at this point and is putty in her hands. The final words in this scene echo the theme of deception established in earlier scenes. After attempting and failing to stand up to his wife, he says: "False face must hide what the false heart doth know". This last line of the scene furthers the theme of **appearance versus reality**.

Act 2 Scene 1

Here we have another scene that tells us a lot about the characters and the atmosphere through the language Shakespeare uses and also through contrast. Banquo and Fleance are up and awake in the courtyard on a starless night. The way things are in the natural world reflects the state in the play because evil has taken hold. On more than one occasion Lady Macbeth and Macbeth himself call for the stars not to shine light upon their deeds, they call on the darkness to hide their intentions. The fact that now the stars are hidden suggests that a course of action has been decided on and cannot be reversed.

Banquo admits that he is having trouble sleeping and this shows us that he, like Macbeth, has been troubled by the witches' prophecies. However, in contrast to Macbeth and especially Lady Macbeth, Banquo looks to the "merciful powers" to help him rather than the evil spirits. Another contrast is between Banquo and Duncan. Whereas Duncan was effusive in his praise and lavish in his compliments when he arrives at Macbeth's castle, Banquo is on guard and on edge. He asks for his sword when he hears someone approaching. This is significant because he is in a friend's castle where, supposedly, no harm can come to him. This tells us that Banquo is suspicious or fears something occurring. He also asks "who's there?" This can be read simply as him calling out to see who's approaching or also as him trying to get Macbeth to identify his real self. We've seen all the metaphors Shakespeare uses about hidden identity and showing "false face" and now Banquo is calling on Macbeth to reveal himself.

There is an interesting discussion between the two when Macbeth suggests something without actually saying it. He says: "If you shall cleave to my consent when 'tis, it shall make honour for you". Here it's as if he's subtly hinting at some event to come in the future. He's essentially telling Banquo that if he sticks with him when the time comes, that he'll get something out of it. Banquo's response is equally mysterious but also telling. He says: "So I lose none in seeking to augment it, but still keep my bosom franchised and allegiance clear, I shall be counselled." Here, his response is: so long as I don't lose any honour or have to change my allegiance to the king then I'll listen to what you have to say.

Another key part of this scene (and some of the most famous lines from the play) sees Macbeth preparing to do the unthinkable: "Is this a dagger I see before me..." Macbeth, who has already decided to kill Duncan, shows the audience his troubled state of mind by describing the hallucination of the bloodied dagger leading him towards Duncan's room. It's important not to confuse this hallucination as a prompt toward the act of killing. Macbeth has already decided to murder the king and even says that the dagger is pointing him "the way that I was going". This hallucination is simply a symptom of a fevered mind and shows the audience the mental pressure that Macbeth is under. It's a product of his imagination designed to show the audience that he has fully decided on this path.

Act 2 Scene 2

Another of the **key questions** surrounding this play is whether or not we feel sorry for Macbeth. He is a noble and well-respected man. He is brave, loyal and courageous in battle. He is ambitious but, through the actions of an evil woman (or women if you consider the witches), he pushes that ambition too far. Ultimately, he sees the errors of his ways and he falls from his position. Considering this, is it possible to feel some sympathy for him?

On the other hand, however, he is a brutal killer who decapitates people at the behest of the king. He schemes and plots with his wife and the witches to murder a good and noble man. He goes against all decency and moral principle by killing his king, his relative and a guest in his own home. He also kills many more people indiscriminately in order to keep his ill-gotten gains. In this light, is it much more difficult to feel sorry for him?

This scene is one of the keys to unlocking this debate. The fact that the murder of Duncan occurs offstage is significant because it would be very difficult, if not impossible, for the audience to have a shred of sympathy for Macbeth if they were to witness the actual act. The first we actually see of Macbeth following the deed is when he returns, still holding the bloody daggers. Macbeth says: "I have done the deed" while Lady Macbeth, seeing he's brought the murder weapons with him, says: "Why did you bring the daggers from the place? They must lie there."

Macbeth is full of fear, almost hysterically so, as well as remorse and sadness for what he has done. The fact that we see the state of Macbeth after the murder rather than the deed itself is important to how we feel toward Macbeth as a character. We also feel an amount of sympathy for Lady

Macbeth when she admits that she had tried to murder Duncan but he "resembled my father as he slept" so she couldn't bring herself to do it. This is the only human emotion we see in Lady Macbeth in the whole play.

The confidence and mastery of language and argument displayed by both characters is completely absent in this scene. Both of them are on edge and Lady Macbeth, in particular, is troubled by her husband's reaction to the murder. She jumps at the sound of an owl "hark! peace!" while Macbeth behaves as if in a trance. He appears not to care whether he is caught or not and indulges in self-reproach while Lady Macbeth desperately tries to bring him round.

One of the most famous ironies of the play is introduced here. Lady Macbeth urges her husband to wash the blood from his hands telling him "a little water clears us of this deed". This is an extended metaphor that we see in the rest of the play in many ways where the image of blood and water is used to show that murderous deeds are impossible to wash away. Lady Macbeth herself returns to this image when she is close to insane.

There is a real contrast between both characters in this scene. While both are on edge and both appear painfully human, it is Lady Macbeth's practical side, which is called into operation. Macbeth's remorse at the killing has left him in a state where he could easily be detected. He has brought the daggers with him from the room, a metaphor perhaps of his guilt, which requires Lady Macbeth to return them, thus exposing her to the crime and a vision that, later in the play, haunts her dreams.

The knocking at the gate is symbolic in a number of ways. The audience as well as the characters have been in this grim, ghoulish and dark environment for a number of scenes. We've been exposed to Macbeth's fevered ramblings and Lady Macbeth's cold calculations. The knocking symbolises the reality outside of the castle gates. There is a world out there not immediately poisoned by these deeds. It's also a symbol, extended in the following scene, of the knocking at the gates of hell. In Act 1 when Lady Macbeth dedicated herself to evil and, in effect, is possessed by demons, her castle becomes a type of hell. She leads Duncan by the hand into this hell and he never emerges. The stars over the castle don't shine and, as we will see in later scenes, the murder of Duncan disrupts the balance in **nature**.

The knocking wakes Macbeth and Lady Macbeth from the dark and murderous reverie in which they've held the audience and it suddenly makes the deed they've committed shocking, raw and real.

Act 2 Scene 3

This scene can be interpreted in a number of ways but either way, the use of **language** and **structure** is very important. Firstly, it is often described as a bit of 'comic relief' where Shakespeare releases the tension built up over the previous scenes and, especially in light of the scenes immediately before. Scenes of comic relief were traditionally there so as to give the audience something to laugh at before again building up the tension in the play. It is questionable, however, as to why Shakespeare would need this. He has spent the previous Act and scenes carefully building up the tension so it wouldn't make a great deal of sense to introduce humour here.

There is much that the drunk porter says in this scene that reflects the actual events on the other side of the gate. The images he uses and the themes of his speech are ones we see often throughout the play. The porter mentions a number of events and characters, all of which would have been to familiar to Shakespeare's audience as they were current events at the time. The common thread between them all is that the characters in the stories he tells committed deeds that would condemn them to hell.

First there is the farmer who keeps all his grain to himself when other people are starving because he thinks it will make it more valuable and he'll get a better price for it. The next harvest, however, is plentiful and the price of his grain plummets and ruins him. The next character is the equivocator and this is interesting because it relates to the theme of truth and deception in the play. This part of the scene could refer to an actual equivocator, Father Garnet, who was involved in the Gunpowder Plot (a plot to kill the king in Shakespeare's time) and was tried for treason. He told half-truths and attempted to get out of trouble through his use of clever language. He was, however, hanged for perjury (lying under oath). The porter says that you can't equivocate your way into heaven and, in this case, out of hell.

After the Porter exits, we are met with Macbeth who has had time to wash his hands and change his clothes. There is an interesting detail in both the language and the structure here. When speaking with Macduff and Lennox, Macbeth responds in short, brief sentences. This is at odds with the Macbeth we have met so far who speaks in great long monologues and soliloquies using language that is heavy with imagery, metaphors and symbolism. Now, however, we have Macbeth saying "Good morrow both... Not yet... I'll bring you to him..." when he is asked questions.

Shakespeare is using Macbeth's language as a reflection of his state of mind. In all his speech here, he must be very careful about what he is saying. He must either equivocate or lie outright and thus, his speech becomes slow, brief and thought out. It's only after the discovery of Duncan's body that he can again speak naturally. In an interesting way, there's an interpretation here that Macbeth's words and feelings in the aftermath of the discovery are the only time in the whole play where he is not hiding how he feels or trying to deceive anyone. He says: "Had I but died an hour before this chance, I had lived a blessed time". This is completely true. Up until the point where he murders Duncan, he is living a blessed life. He is respected, well looked after and happy. From this point on, however, he is doomed.

The murder of the grooms or the two servants is interesting too. Macbeth very eloquently describes why he did it and it marks a departure from his original plan. As he said in Act 1, committing murder creates more bloodshed, he has now murdered three people where the plan involved just one. His defence of this appears thought out rather than impulsive and there is a very interesting shift in this scene between Lady Macbeth and her husband.

For the first time, Macbeth seems to be the one in control and creating practical solutions to problems while Lady Macbeth appears to give in to her emotions, and faints.

Act 2 Scene 4

In Shakespeare's time it was believed that there was a **natural order** into which everything fell. Just as there was an order in the animal world, there was also one amongst men. At the top was God's representative on earth: the king. Under him were various noblemen, lords, gentry (land owners) and at the bottom, peasants and slaves. It was believed that any break in this order was reflected elsewhere, a sign of how serious it was to upset the natural order of things.

One of the most significant upsets to this order was regicide or the killing of the king. This is just what Macbeth does and, eventually, he himself becomes king. In order for the play to reach its conclusion, he must be removed and a rightful heir must take his place as king and return the natural order to a state of balance.

In this scene we have The Old Man and Ross discussing the happenings in the play from outside the main character's points of view. They talk about the disturbances in nature: how a "mousing owl" caught and killed a "falcon". This would be unnatural because a falcon would be above an owl in the natural order of the animal kingdom.

Shakespeare is using images of a disturbance in nature to reflect the huge crime done against Duncan. It is a crime that is so significant it has affected the balance of nature. The language and structure here in this scene is significant because of the way The Old Man speaks. He uses natural and sincere language; he is superstitious and simple-minded. Ross, on the other hand, speaks in an almost artificial way. This is brought into perspective when he speaks with Macduff.

Ross admits his intention to follow the story being put about by Macbeth that Duncan's sons murdered their father and he will go to Scone to see Macbeth crowned King. Macduff, however, signals his uncertainty by saying that he will go home to Fife. Ross understands that the story they are being told is likely to be untrue but he is following it because he is uncertain of what may happen; Macbeth is not the only one who hides what he knows.

Act 3 Scene 1

The scenes that involve Macbeth following the murder of Duncan can be seen as each representing a new low in his descent into darkness and evil. Here, shortly after murdering his king, he is already plotting to murder his close friend Banquo.

It is Banquo's turn to use soliloquy in this scene and he does so to suggest that he is not altogether comfortable with how Macbeth has come to the throne. Just like Ross in the previous scene, there are a few characters who do not entirely believe that Macbeth didn't kill Duncan but are choosing not to speak out - either to see what they might get under the new king or through fear.

Banquo epitomises this uncertainty as, in his soliloquy, he appears to be suggesting that he's not best pleased with how Macbeth has won the throne, "I fear thou play'dst most foully for't," but thinks that it may lead to something for him "May they not be my oracles as well". Banquo has played the loyal subject with Duncan and with Macbeth. The events in the rest of this scene could be interpreted as Macbeth fearing a man loyal to a dead king or, alternatively, a man loyal to no king, who will do anything to further his own means.

One of the most pleasing things about this play is the richness of language. Shakespeare enhances his words with **double-meanings, puns and irony** creating an environment for the audience where they are on edge. Every thing said could mean something other that the intended meaning. It adds to the tension in the play and creates deep uncertainty. In this scene, for example, Macbeth's opening words are "Here's our chief guest". Considering the fact that Duncan was the chief guest recently, this can be seen in a number of different ways. In fact, it turns out that Macbeth does indeed plan to kill Banquo and, as such, we can see that to be Macbeth's "chief guest" is not a good thing at all.

Throughout the play Macbeth's speech changes in order to reflect his state of mind. We see him reacting to different situations by adjusting his speech. The Macbeth we have here in this scene is also quite a different man to previous scenes. As detailed earlier, we've seen Macbeth the soldier, Macbeth the worrier, Macbeth the private man, Macbeth the morose and now, most chillingly of all, we have the cunning, devious and evil Macbeth. **Language** is a marker of both status and also state-of-mind.

At this point in the play, there doesn't appear to be much difference between Macbeth and his wife. He is so calculating about the way he places his questions that Banquo doesn't suspect a thing: "Ride you this afternoon?", "Is't far you ride?", "Goes Fleance with you?". These questions betray to the audience the plan in place but not to Banquo, an excellent example of **dramatic irony**.

Some of the final words spoken between the pair are interesting in that there are multiple interpretations. Macbeth says to Banquo: "Fail not our feast". Now, Macbeth has plotted to have Banquo murdered and knows already that he will fail to make the feast. Macbeth is slipping into evil here, into the type of language used by his wife and the witches. Banquo's response is interesting too. He says "My Lord I will not" which we can interpret as a basic response to a request from the king but also, the irony is that he actually does make the feast, albeit in the form of a ghost of Macbeth's imagination.

Another snapshot of Macbeth becoming more like his wife is shown to the audience when he is speaking with the murderers. Gone is Macbeth's noble and considered speech, now he is cajoling and cunning just as his wife was when she urged him to kill Duncan. He appeals to the men's self-esteem and also to their manhood in order to persuade them to kill Banquo. Macbeth says: "If you have a station in the file, Not i' the worst rank of manhood, say it".

It is interesting to wonder whether this was the true Macbeth all along or if this is some sort of mania brought on by the murder of his King. It appears that he is taking over Lady Macbeth's role and revelling in it. Is this a case of the mask slipping to reveal the true man or is it just one of many masks and Macbeth is simply getting carried away? By reversing the roles over the course of the play, is Shakespeare giving us a comment about how evil deeds corrupt the person who does them?

Act 3 Scene 2

Here we have a brief scene between Macbeth and Lady Macbeth. What's significant about this scene is that it shows us the state of their relationship and also, it shows us how the roles have reversed between them. Lady Macbeth is beginning to feel the strain of their deed. She realises that they've done something terrible but neither of them are secure and happy "Nought's had, all's spent...". Unconsciously from the point of view of the characters but in a very deliberate ploy from Shakespeare, the soliloquies and worries begin to echo each other. Macbeth is concerned in the previous scene that, even though he has killed Duncan, he is not "safely thus". Macbeth begins to worry that they've done it all for nothing. Lady Macbeth begins to worry about precisely the same thing.

They are both, however, trying to hide their worry and misery from each other. Macbeth refuses to let Lady Macbeth in on the plan in advance "Be innocent of the knowledge, dearest chuck", to try to protect her while she rebukes him for being miserable, telling him "what's done is done". Both of them are struggling to sleep, suffering "terrible dreams" and "torture of the mind". It is clear that both characters are experiencing the same thing, they need each other. What happens, however, is that they begin to drift apart. Now, Lady Macbeth comes to her husband asking "what's to be done?".

After he hides the plan to murder Banquo from his wife, their relationship never really recovers. He has locked out his partner in crime and assumed her role. She is now dependent on him for guidance and, while he still needs her to confess his secrets, the "scorpions" of the mind, he does not need her for anything else. She does recover some of her former sternness briefly in the banquet scene but the Lady Macbeth of Act 2 is now gone. Instead, we have in her a case study in how evil deeds can ruin a person. Remember, she had called on evil to fill up her body so, to all intents and purposes, she is possessed by demons.

Act 3 Scene 3

Macbeth has planned to kill both Banquo and Fleance because the witches told them that Banquo's sons would be kings. The simple fact that Macbeth plots their murders shows the audience that Macbeth is challenging fate, the same fate that brought him the title of Cawdor and the crown. He trusts fate to give him titles but doesn't believe that it will do the same for others. It's also clear from the witches' prophecies that the real danger from the two is Fleance. Banquo will not be king, only his sons will be.

This murder scene, then, is significant for two reasons. Firstly, Macbeth sends a third murderer after the other two to make sure that the job is done correctly. This shows a complete lack of trust in anything and anyone. Macbeth wants to be doubly sure. Also, even with the three murderers, Fleance lives. Later, the second murderer says: "We have lost the best half of our affair" meaning that Fleance, the real threat to Macbeth, has escaped.

The scene shows us that Macbeth is happy to believe in fate in one instance and then try to change it in the next. He is inconsistent and changeable. He believes what he wants to believe. This may be the sign of a weak or immature character and certainly not of a clever and noble man. Again, this brings into focus the question of whether or not we feel sympathy for this character.

He was perfectly correct in his prediction that bloody deeds cause more bloody deeds and here he is now paying murderers to kill his friends. This is despite the fact that, if he believes in the same fate that has brought him to this point, it is completely useless. Does this make him a monster? Which is worse - him killing Banquo to try to hold on to the throne despite knowing it's impossible or killing Banquo in some hope that he can win out over fate?

Act 3 Scene 4

Remember Banquo's words when Macbeth said "Fail not our feast". In Shakespeare's plays, feasts are symbols of social harmony and kinship. This feast is supposed to be Macbeth's celebration feast. No matter how he came to the throne, this banquet is his chance to endear himself to his society and to make his kingship respectable. We see both Macbeth and Lady Macbeth going overboard in their effort to make everyone welcome: "The hearty welcome", "We will require her welcome", "They are welcome", "Be large in mirth" and "love and health to all".

This is Macbeth's chance to put all of the bad deeds to rest and become a good king. Banquets and feasts are such a powerful metaphor that what comes next is very significant. Firstly, the murderer arrives with his face smeared with blood. This can be read as a symbol that Macbeth can't hide the evil that he has indulged in to get this far. Even a man's best kept secrets will come out. The fact that the murderer enters just as everyone has been seated for the feast is important. Macbeth is unable to sit with his guests just as he is unable to stand alongside them in society.

After Macbeth returns from speaking with the murderer who has told him that Banquo is dead, he finds his seat taken by Banquo's bloody ghost. This scene is rich both in drama and dramatic irony. Macbeth is confronted by an apparition that only he can see: a symptom of his guilt. He panics, becomes hysterical and upsets all of his guests. Lady Macbeth, in her last act of taking charge, tries to allay the guests' fears by telling them that he sometimes behaves like this, it is nothing and not to worry. "Sit, worthy friends", she tells them. "My lord is often thus and hath been from his youth."

Aside from the drama of Macbeth hallucinating in front of his guests, we also have the dramatic irony of Macbeth returning from conspiring with Banquo's murderer to find Banquo's ghost sitting in the king's seat. This echoes the prophecy from the witches that Banquo's sons will come to the throne. For all his efforts, Macbeth's feast ends in complete disorder and disarray. This is symbolic of how he has tried to get people on his side, to bring his society together, and failed spectacularly. The reason for his failure is the deeds that he has committed to get to this point.

It has been said previously by both Macbeth and Lady Macbeth that the best thing would be if they could just kill Duncan and that would be the end of it, then they could be a good king and queen. The death toll is rising, however, and Macbeth's poisoned mind is starting to betray him. For all his desire to fit in with the nobles and lords in his society, Macbeth's behaviour in this scene completely alienates him and, after this point, he begins to crumble and feel that he is alone in the world.

This scene also acts as another waypoint in the ever-changing relationship between Macbeth and his wife. She tries to rally round him at the beginning, telling the guests not to worry about her husband's strange behaviour but, by the end, she has told everyone to leave and she herself is strangely quiet. It's as if the mental strain of "showing false face" which she advised her husband to do repeatedly, is exhausting her. Finally, with her spirit broken, she responds briefly and without excitement when Macbeth tells her of his further plans. She is beyond caring now and the only time we see her after this point is in the sleepwalking scene when we see the full torment her mind is going through.

Macbeth, on the other hand, appears to be growing in his role as the murderous king. He talks, albeit wearily, about the need for further murders. From the point where Lady Macbeth urged him to kill Duncan, he has now taken the initiative and he is in full charge of what they do after this point. Here we have a very important image and metaphor from Shakespeare. He talks about the river of blood, how he has murdered so many people and done so much evil, "I am in blood, stepped in so far", that it doesn't make much different whether he stops now or continues on his current path, "that should I wade no more, returning were as tedious as to go o'er".

This is yet another side to Macbeth. Here we have a man who his wife urged to "become a man" not long ago behaving as if murder is something small and meaningless. As he has grown in terms of his murderous nature, Lady Macbeth has shrunk. He has taken from her the evil he needed to block out his noble nature. His relationship with his wife, it appears, has completely collapsed. There is nothing between them now.

Act 3 Scene 5

Many scholars and editors believe that this scene as not actually written by Shakespeare at all but inserted by actors either to give themselves more lines or to excite the audience, for whom scenes of witches and witchcraft and the supernatural would have been very popular. Much of the evidence for this comes from the fact that Hecate has so many lines despite not being introduced at any point previously. It is also said that the witches appear different to what they were when we first meet them.

At the beginning, the witches appear to treat Macbeth as the poor victim of their scheming and plotting but here they treat him almost as if he is one of their own. This could either be because, as suggested, it was written by someone else or it could also reflect how far into his evil nature Macbeth has travelled. Maybe they treat him as one of their own because he has shown just how evil he has been.

There is, however, some element of value to the final words Hecate speaks when she talks about how Macbeth's over-confidence will have an impact on his actions and, thus, have a bearing on the rest of the play. Again, Shakespeare is using the technique of **foreshadowing** or **echoing** to give the readers hints about what is to come.

Act 3 Scene 6

In Shakespeare's day, the idea of regicide was so shocking that, even in a play, Shakespeare has to be careful to give very good reasons for the removal of a king. Even in this case, where we have a king who murdered his own predecessor, he is still the lawfully crowned king and Shakespeare must be very careful. It is also worth mentioning that he would often have had kings and members of the royal family at his theatre watching the play so he had to be very careful not to offend.

This scene then is a way for other characters to set out the reasons why Macbeth must be removed from the throne. The subjects, in this case Lennox, give a commentary of how people in general feel about Macbeth as king and the state of the country. This scene also leads neatly into the fact that Macduff is in England seeking the help of the king there to remove Macbeth. This, in turn, leads to Macbeth preparing to move against Macduff's family - an act which almost makes it impossible for us to have any sympathy for him.

This scene also gives Macbeth, if he needed any, a reason to kill Macduff's family. It acts as a structural feature for Shakespeare in order to give context to the story, a reason for Macbeth to be killed and also as a device to bring the audience out of the claustrophobic mind of Macbeth and back into the "reality" of the play.

Act 4 Scene 1

Back to the witches. This scene furthers the theme of deception and equivocation in the play. As we have seen throughout Macbeth, appearance versus reality is an important aspect of each of the characters. Many of the characters wear metaphorical masks and speak in half-truths, none more so than the witches.

At the beginning of the scene, the witches are putting all sorts of hideous ingredients into their cauldron. This is almost an echo of Macbeth's banquet where everything fell apart and ended in ruin. Here, the witches are preparing their own special feast, which reflects the evil that has been done in the play. Macbeth approaches the witches full of bravado and confidence, echoing Hecate's prophecy in Act 3 Scene 5 that Macbeth's over-confidence would bring his downfall.

Shakespeare also uses another **structural device** here in this scene. Macbeth has come looking for reassurance and comfort that what he has done will keep him on the throne. The witches duly show him three apparitions, which Macbeth interprets in his own way. These apparitions, while seeming to comfort him, are actually entirely deceptive and symptomatic of how the witches speak - in riddles and half-truths. The audience are shown a series of apparitions that are supposed to confirm one thing, but in fact can be interpreted as the complete opposite. Shakespeare is flagging something that becomes crucial to the final outcome of the play. He is, in a way, signposting important details for his audience.

The first of the apparitions is the armed head and literally foretells Macbeth's eventual decapitation at the hands of Macduff. Macbeth, however, appears to believe that the head is representative of Macduff and he seems thankful having seen it, obviously misunderstanding its true meaning.

The second vision is of the bloody child, which is, in reality, Macduff. The advice given to Macbeth is that he should feel completely safe and secure because no one who hasn't been "born of woman" can hurt him. The equivocation here is that the apparition *is* Macduff and so clearly, he is alive despite not being born of woman. Macbeth fails to see the deception here and he reads into the prophecy that he has nothing to fear.

The third vision is of Malcolm, Duncan's son, coming to Macbeth's castle carrying a branch from a tree. The advice here again is that Macbeth can't be harmed until Birnam Wood moves to Dunsinane. Obviously believing that it is impossible for a forest to move, he feels even more secure following this prophecy. Essentially, Macbeth has come to the witches for reassurance; they've shown him a vision of the future, and he has read into it *what he wants* to see so he goes away completely reassured.

Before he leaves, however, the witches, on his orders, show him a final vision. Here he sees a line of eight kings who are all descendants of Banquo. This leaves him in an awful state considering that it means no one descended from him will inherit the throne. It's very curious here that Macbeth sees this and, yet still doesn't doubt the earlier prophecies. It's clear the witches are playing with him yet, in his state, he either doesn't seem to notice or care.

The final part of this scene is crucial to the development of Macbeth's character. So far, he has killed a number of people but each murder, one could argue, had its purpose. Before killing Duncan and Banquo he argued with himself, went through their good qualities and ultimately decided that murder had to be done. Here, however, he decides on murder with no qualms or counsel. He says that from here on out he won't hesitate: once he has thought of an act, he will carry it out. He says: "From this moment the very firstlings of my heart shall be the firstlings of my hand". He plots to murder Macduff's wife and children in a terrible act that almost dehumanises him in our eyes. It's difficult to have any sympathy for him or to see him as anything other than a monster.

Act 4 Scene 2

This scene is terrible because, throughout we are waiting for something bad to happen to Macduff's family. We see more deception here when Lady Macduff tells her son that her father is a traitor and there is an in-depth conversation between mother and son about the nature of treason and who can be declared treasonous.

It's significant that, although we see the boy being murdered, Macbeth himself doesn't carry out the deed. In fact, there is the suggestion that he couldn't have brought himself to do it even if he wanted to. This, I believe, is Macbeth's lowest ebb. He is an out-and-out villain. There is almost nothing positive in him as a character and the only way Shakespeare can keep him some way redeemable is by not having him visually involved in the murder.

As mentioned earlier, Shakespeare needs to keep Macbeth as a character who can arouse some sort of sympathy in the audience or otherwise this isn't a tragic play, just a play about a complete monster whom everyone is glad to see die. So we can see all of Shakespeare's attempts to keep Macbeth away, in the audience's eyes at least, from the murders he sanctions, as structural ploys to maintain some element of sympathy for the central character.

Act 4 Scene 3

This is one of the longest scenes in the play and also quite important for setting up a real alternative to Macbeth, establishing the character who is big enough and strong enough to tackle Macbeth. The discussion that Macduff and Malcolm have here is very long but serves a number of purposes. Again, deception is the name of the game. Malcolm, in contrast to his father, is showing immense caution and testing Macduff to see if he really can trust him. This contrast is important as even Malcolm says: "To show an unfelt sorrow is an office, which the false man does easy".

He's saying that false men find it easy to lie. This is interesting in the case of Macbeth because, as we can remember at the beginning he didn't find it easy to lie at all. His wife chided him for showing his feelings on his face "as a book". Over time however, and with the benefit of practice, Macbeth becomes astute at saying one thing but meaning something completely different.

Malcolm, therefore, is very keen to test Macduff and there is even the suggestion that Macbeth has sent spies before to try to trick Malcolm into coming back to Scotland, where he would most certainly be killed by Macbeth.

As well as showing the contrast between Malcolm and his father, this scene also shows us, through a sort of commentary, all that is wrong in Scotland and also, what a good king should be like. Throughout the exchange between the two, Malcolm denounces himself as being greedy, lustful and violent all in an effort to gauge Macduff's reaction. At the end, when Malcolm says that, were he to be king, he would "pour the sweet milk of concord into Hell, uproar the universal peace, confound all unity on earth" Macduff is at his wits' end.

This is a subtle way of describing Scotland's state under Macbeth's rule. As we saw earlier, men's actions can disrupt the natural order, which results in disruptions in nature. Here, Malcolm is describing a country completely ruined and miserable and that is precisely what Macbeth's Scotland is.

Having described, in a roundabout fashion, what an evil king would be like, Malcolm goes on to say that he is none of these things and is, in fact, perfectly fitted to rule. He describes now what a good king should be like and it is notable that he talks about the English king, Edward the Confessor. All his talk about Edward being able to heal people through touch and being a deeply religious man fits in with what people in Shakespearean times thought of kings: they were somehow connected to God and were capable of great deeds and even miracles.

Another interesting sub-plot here is that Shakespeare's benefactor, King James, was a descendant of Edward the confessor so it was very important that Shakespeare showed Edward in a good light. He certainly does in this scene. While Edward is gentle and noble, Macbeth is murderous and barbaric. Edward is religious and performs miracles while Macbeth consorts with witches and is involved with spells and witchcraft. Edward spreads love and harmony, while the air in Scotland is "filthy" and diseased.

Finally, it is in this scene that Macduff learns that his family has been murdered. Here we now have two characters who have been "filled out" enough for the audience to believe and engage in their attempt to recapture the crown from the "tyrant" Macbeth.

Act 5 Scene 1

Here we meet Lady Macbeth once again. We finally see the price that she has to pay for giving up her womanliness and dedicating herself to the "spirits": she has lost her mind. Her loss of reason is remarkable considering how, in earlier scenes, she appears completely untroubled by evil and the supernatural. She told Macbeth in Act 3 that "the dead... are but as pictures". She is telling him to grow up, dead people are just like paintings - they can't hurt you. Now, however, she is completely possessed by guilt and it is causing her to walk and talk in her sleep - a sure sign in Shakespeare's day of possession or madness.

There is another interesting parallel between this scene and when she convinces Macbeth to kill Duncan by attacking his manhood. Macbeth, at one stage, replies to her by saying "I dare do all that may become a man, who dares do more is none". This can be interpreted as Macbeth saying that he is a man - anyone who goes beyond that (by killing his king for example) is not a man because they lose their humanity. Here, it appears that Lady Macbeth is lost. She has gone beyond humanity and the guilt and stress on her mind is simply too great.

There is a very good analogy suggested by D. J. Enright that compares Macbeth and his wife. He suggests that Lady Macbeth is a sprinter in evil while Macbeth is a long-distance runner. He starts off slowly but can go for much longer.

This is reinforced through Shakespeare's use of repetition and imagery in this scene. Lady Macbeth's soliloquy repeatedly focuses on blood and murder. She says such things as "who would have thought the old man to have had so much blood in him", "Here's the smell of the blood still", "The Thane of Fife had a wife..." and "Out, out damned spot..." This is all from the woman who said that simply washing your hands of the blood removes the deed from your mind. She's learning the hard way the toll these deeds have had on her mind.

There is also the potential for alternative interpretation on Shakespeare's use of **language** in the famous lines: "Out, out damned spot...". Firstly, we can assume that she is unable to wash the blood from her hands - a symbol that she is unable to remove the deed from her mind. Another way is, if you go back to Shakespeare's time, that she may be possessed by demons. It was remarked in those days that demons and witches had a spot somewhere upon their bodies, which marked them out as evil. If, as she asked in Act 2, she has been possessed by demons then this would be a symbol that she is trying to get her soul back but, obviously, she has a price to pay for the crimes she has committed.

Lady Macbeth's fate is the final nail in the coffin of her relationship with Macbeth. After she dies, he is utterly alone but there is also a suggestion that he is already alone and that her death means nothing to him. We shall explore this further in scene five.

Act 5 Scene 2

In this scene we see again the **extended metaphor** of attire, clothes and garments not fitting. Angus refers to Macbeth as a dwarf wearing a giant's robes. Again, we can take this to mean that Duncan, as a good king, was a 'giant' while Macbeth, in his place, is a dwarf. I feel this means more about stature rather than any literal sense of size. Certainly as the play draws to its conclusion, we begin to see the final version of Macbeth and he is not shirking or hiding.

Over the next few scenes and here also we get an idea of the forces massing against Macbeth, I think the most interesting part of it is the turmoil he himself faces internally. The building forces outside his castle are almost a mere distraction to his own thoughts. For the audience too, I feel that we are being guided in the direction of Macbeth's own thoughts and feelings rather than putting too great a stock in the battle which is due to happen.

Shakespeare makes another interesting **structural** decision here that enhances the impact of the final scenes. From Act 4 Scene 3 when Macduff and Malcolm decide to join forces to overthrow Macbeth until the end of the play, Shakespeare tends to contrast a scene of the "good guys" planning their attack with a scene where we see Macbeth in emotional turmoil. Through this we see the liberating army steadily moving towards Macbeth's castle while we see Macbeth himself steadily descending into despair.

While Macbeth believes himself to be invincible, we see that his real enemy is his conscience. He is suffering the weight of the decisions he has made and the acts he has carried out. The armies gathering outside his castle are inconsequential, an annoyance at best. The real battle is within his mind and soul.

Act 5 Scene 3

Following Macbeth's internal monologues we can see that the strain is beginning to show. A doctor comes and tells him about Lady Macbeth and how she is suffering but he simply tells him to treat her illness. He invokes an analogy here asking the doctor if he can treat a sick country. This echoes and furthers Shakespeare's **metaphor** from the scene in the English Court when the doctor there tells Malcolm about how King Edward heals and helps the sick people in his country while here in Scotland, we are left to assume, the entire country is sick and it is as a result of Macbeth himself.

He swings through a number of different moods here from rage, disgust to misery and, finally, determination. Macbeth believes that there is still a chance for him and, as such, he decides to face the invaders, single-handedly if required, "till from my bones my flesh be hacked".

Shakespeare is trying his best to get the audience to have some admiration for Macbeth. He is now, logistically speaking, ruined. The armies gathering outside are too great for him to defeat and he is left with only one option – face them like a man, like the great warrior we saw at the beginning.

Act 5 Scene 4

Here Malcolm orders that soldiers are to cut down a bough from the tree and carry it in front of him to disguise their numbers. Macbeth believed wholeheartedly in the witches' prophecies and this is, yet another of them, coming true in an unfortunate way. His bravery and determination at the end of Scene 3 are completely misplaced because they are based on the idea that he invincible, which he is not.

Act 5 Scene 5

Macbeth hears of his wife's death and responds by saying that she should have "died hereafter". There are two ways of interpreting this line. Either Macbeth means she would have died anyway which would symbolise the complete breakdown of their relationship - her dying is almost an annoyance, a distraction as he is planning for battle or he means she shouldn't have died yet, it should have been at a later date. This second interpretation doesn't necessarily mean that their relationship was a bed of roses but it's still better than the first.

This scene is notable for Macbeth's soliloquy. It is one of the best-known speeches in all of Shakespeare's work and it is incredibly moving. Having just heard of his wife's death, Macbeth considers what's left of his own life. He speaks about the trivial nature of life, how it's essentially worthless because all people do is "creep" from day to day until, eventually, they die. He paints people as fools and idiots, playing parts and lying to themselves about the true nature of life.

This is one of Shakespeare's most impressive speeches as it is rich with imagery and metaphor. In fact, many of the extended metaphors he uses throughout the play appear to tie together neatly in this speech. The imagery of clothing, of falsehood, of appearance versus reality, of daggers covered in blood and painted pictures are all, in one sense, part of the theatre and this soliloquy uses the theatre as a metaphor for life - how people play their "part", tread the stage and then die.

Shakespeare gives us the image of people scrambling around in the dark with candles, trying to find their way "...lighted fools the way to dusty death". We pity them because they are fools. All of human effort and achievement are simply shadows thrown by the candles, and the acting he does is only a version of reality. Life, Macbeth tells us, is just a story, told by an idiot and it means absolutely nothing.

This is deeply depressing stuff and, when he is interrupted by the messenger telling him that Birnam Wood is moving, we see Macbeth, finally, completely stripped of all his self-confidence and assurances. The truth of his situation becomes apparent to him. He realises that the witches have deceived him, that he has killed his king, his friends and possibly his wife, for nothing. It is a very painful moment for the audience as, instead of feeling satisfaction at his realisation, we feel pity. In fact, Shakespeare has worked hard throughout the play to ensure that we can pity him and especially here at the end of this scene.

Despite knowing that it's all futile, that he has been tricked and that life, as he described it, is just white noise with no meaning, he refuses to yield. This refusal to give in is what gives him back some of his former glory. He stands up against the "petty pace from day to day" and cries "no" to fate. He is alone against the tide of soldiers outside his castle and he is prepared to see it through to the end. Regardless of how he got here, his principles at this point are admirable.

Act 5 Scene 6 & 7

In Scene 6 the battle begins when the troops throw down their branches and then, in scene 7 Macbeth joins the fray. He is determined and fierce and Shakespeare gives us the image of a bear tied to a stake pursued by savage dogs. This is what Macbeth thinks of his enemies. He also has some last bit of confidence, as he has not yet figured out the true meaning of the witches' prophecy about Macduff, being "not of woman born".

When Macbeth faces young Siward, Siward hopes to kill Macbeth and make a name for himself. Macbeth, returning to the warrior that we met at the very beginning, kills him easily. This, in contrast to the other killings in the play, is a honourable death for Siward. As his father says at the end, his wounds were in his front so he can't have any complaints.

This echoes another theme in the play, that of valour and bravery in a violent and vicious world. The world that the play is set in is dangerous and violent. Macbeth is heralded at the beginning of the play for killing lots of people but it is acceptable because they are the "enemies" of Scotland. When he goes on killing people, the wrong sort of people, then people become concerned. He is no less or more a killer at the beginning than at the end, it's simply that he has upset the natural order of the society in which he lived.

Finally, in Scene 7, there is a suggestion that Macbeth's soldiers are either not fighting very hard or have completely abandoned him and joined the other side. Malcolm says: "We have met with foes that strike beside us". This emphasises how alone Macbeth is now. It really is him against the world.

Act 5 Scene 8

Finally, the showdown. Macduff and Macbeth face off. Macbeth appears to scorn the idea of suicide - he says "Why should I play the Roman fool and die on mine own sword?" The fact that he says this may suggest that he has thought of this as an idea but he decides, instead, to kill as many enemies as he possibly can.

When he faces Macduff, there is something of the old Macbeth left. He feels immense guilt at killing Macduff's family and attempts to fob him off by telling him that he doesn't want to shed any more of his blood. He also still believes that he can't be defeated by anyone born of a woman and, as such, has misplaced confidence. It is in this scene that he uncovers the final deception, that Macduff was cut from his mother's womb rather than born naturally. This is devastating for Macbeth - understandably so as this is the sole thing on which his confidence was based.

Interestingly, Macbeth's first instinct when faced with this news is to run. He tells Macduff he won't fight him "I'll not fight with thee" but after he is goaded by Macduff he becomes the warrior Macbeth that we know from the opening of the play and he chooses to die fighting rather than to be captured and humiliated. It is interesting that he has to be taunted and almost bullied into doing things in the play. First Lady Macbeth and now Macduff has to force him, through insults, to fight him.

This is the final scene for Macbeth. He has gone through many changes throughout the play and, to be honest, is one of the few characters that Shakespeare presents in any sort of detail. He was feted as Scotland's best warrior; celebrated by his king and loved and respected by his peers. Through ambition, weakness and the influence of others, he threw it all away. He lost parts of his humanity, carried out horrific acts to try to hold on to the slippery semblance of power and, ultimately, ended up completely alone to face his own death.

It's for the audience to decide if they can have any sympathy for him at the end and a key part of that debate lies in the question of whether he was wholly responsible for his own actions? What part did Lady Macbeth play? What about the witches? Were they facilitators or simply bystanders?

Act 5 Scene 9

The king is dead, long live the king! Macbeth has been killed, his head cut off and now everyone gathers round to celebrate. Considering the emotion and tension in the build up to the previous scene, this final scene is very difficult to find entertaining or engaging in any sense. It's clear that the driving force for the whole play is its namesake and, without him, it becomes pedestrian.

The only notable thing about this scene is that order has been restored. This natural order that we met earlier was disrupted by Macbeth and now that he has been removed and Malcolm has become king, or at least is about to become king, everything has been put right. In the last words of the play Macbeth is referred to as a "butcher" Lady Macbeth as his "fiend-like queen" proving a complete and total contrast to how he is introduced at the beginning.

Act 1 Scene 1

ORIGINAL TEXT	MODERN TRANSLATION
A desert place.	**An open place**
Thunder and lightning. Enter three Witches	*Thunder and lightning. Enter three Witches*
First Witch When shall we three meet again In thunder, lightning, or in rain?	**First Witch** When will the three of us meet again Will it be during thunder, lightning or when it's raining?
Second Witch When the hurlyburly's done, When the battle's lost and won.	**Second Witch** When this storm is finished, When the battle is over.
Third Witch That will be ere the set of sun.	**Third Witch** That will be before the sun sets.
First Witch Where the place?	**First Witch** At which place?
Second Witch Upon the heath.	**Second Witch** In an open field.
Third Witch There to meet with Macbeth.	**Third Witch** There we will meet Macbeth.
First Witch I come, Graymalkin!	**First Witch** I'm coming grey cat!
Second Witch Paddock calls.	**Second Witch** The toad, Paddock, is calling.
Third Witch Anon.	**Third Witch** At once! We are coming.
ALL Fair is foul, and foul is fair: Hover through the fog and filthy air.	**ALL** Everything that is bad is good and everything that is good is bad: Let's fly through the fog and dirty air.
Exeunt	*Exeunt*

ORIGINAL TEXT	MODERN TRANSLATION
A camp near Forres.	**An army camp near Forres.**
Alarum within. Enter DUNCAN, MALCOLM, DONALBAIN, LENNOX, with Attendants, meeting a bleeding Sergeant	*Sound of a battle trumpet from offstage. Enter DUNCAN, MALCOLM, DONALBAIN, LENNOX, with servants, meeting a bleeding Sergeant.*
DUNCAN What bloody man is that? He can report, As seemeth by his plight, of the revolt The newest state.	**DUNCAN** Who is that covered in blood? Judging by the bad condition he's in, he can give us the most recent news of the rebellion.
MALCOLM This is the sergeant Who like a good and hardy soldier fought 'Gainst my captivity. Hail, brave friend! Say to the king the knowledge of the broil As thou didst leave it.	**MALCOLM** This is the sergeant Who like a good and brave soldier fought to prevent me being captured. Hello, my brave friend! Tell the king what you know about the battle From when you left it.
Sergeant Doubtful it stood; As two spent swimmers, that do cling together And choke their art. The merciless Macdonwald-- Worthy to be a rebel, for to that The multiplying villanies of nature Do swarm upon him--from the western isles Of kerns and gallowglasses is supplied; And fortune, on his damned quarrel smiling, Show'd like a rebel's whore: but all's too weak: For brave Macbeth--well he deserves that name-- Disdaining fortune, with his brandish'd steel, Which smoked with bloody execution, Like valour's minion carved out his passage Till he faced the slave; Which ne'er shook hands, nor bade farewell to him,	**Sergeant** The battle was undecided; Both sides were like two exhausted swimmers, who cling on to each other Not letting either swim. The merciless Macdonwald, who deserves to be called a rebel because he attracts all natural evils and is being supplied with light-armed soldiers and heavy-armed horsemen from Ireland and the Hebrides; And lady luck, smiling on the rebels' cause at first, decided to abandon them like a fickle prostitute: but Macdonwald, along with luck was not strong enough: For brave Macbeth – he deserves the name – laughed at lady luck with his outstretched sword, Which steamed with the blood of those he had killed, Like the special favourite of courage carved out a pathway through the men Until he faced Macdonwald; Who didn't have time to shake his hand or say goodbye to him,

Till he unseam'd him from the nave to the chaps,
And fix'd his head upon our battlements.

DUNCAN
O valiant cousin! worthy gentleman!

Sergeant
As whence the sun 'gins his reflection
Shipwrecking storms and direful thunders break,
So from that spring whence comfort seem'd to come
Discomfort swells. Mark, king of Scotland, mark:
No sooner justice had with valour arm'd
Compell'd these skipping kerns to trust their heels,
But the Norweyan lord surveying vantage,

With furbish'd arms and new supplies of men
Began a fresh assault.

DUNCAN
Dismay'd not this
Our captains, Macbeth and Banquo?

Sergeant
Yes;
As sparrows eagles, or the hare the lion.

If I say sooth, I must report they were
As cannons overcharged with double cracks, so they
Doubly redoubled strokes upon the foe:
Except they meant to bathe in reeking wounds,

Or memorise another Golgotha,

I cannot tell.
But I am faint, my gashes cry for help.

DUNCAN
So well thy words become thee as thy wounds;
They smack of honour both. Go get him surgeons.

Exit Sergeant, attended

Who comes here?

Before he cut him open from the belly to the jaw,
And put his head upon our castle walls.

DUNCAN
O well done sir! You've fought bravely!

Sergeant
Just like when calm seas can suddenly be transformed by thunder storms that can wreck ships,
Just when we thought the battle was won
There came more trouble. Listen, King of Scotland, listen:

No sooner had we, with all our military might, sent all these lightly armed soldiers fleeing,

When the Norwegian King, seeing an advantage now that we were tired,
With new supplies of men and weapons
Began to attack us.

DUNCAN
Did this not frighten the two captains of our army, Macbeth and Banquo?

Sergeant
Yes;
Just as the sparrows frighten eagles, or hares frighten lions.
If I say so, I must report that they were
Like cannons with twice as much gunpowder in them as normal and they attacked the Norwegians twice as hard as the rebels:
It appeared as if they wanted to bathe in the blood they were spilling,
Or recreate another scene as memorable as Golgotha, where Christ was crucified,
I'm not sure.
But I'm feeling faint now, I need help with my wounds.

DUNCAN
Your words are as impressive as your wounds;
They are both a sign of honour. Go get him a surgeon.

Exit Sergeant, attended

Who's there?

Enter ROSS

MALCOLM
The worthy thane of Ross.

LENNOX
What a haste looks through his eyes! So should he look
That seems to speak things strange.

ROSS
God save the king!

DUNCAN
Whence camest thou, worthy thane?

ROSS
From Fife, great king;
Where the Norweyan banners flout the sky

And fan our people cold. Norway himself,

With terrible numbers,
Assisted by that most disloyal traitor
The thane of Cawdor, began a dismal conflict;

Till that Bellona's bridegroom, lapp'd in proof,
Confronted him with self-comparisons,
Point against point rebellious, arm 'gainst arm.

Curbing his lavish spirit: and, to conclude,

The victory fell on us.

DUNCAN
Great happiness!

ROSS
That now
Sweno, the Norways' king, craves composition:

Nor would we deign him burial of his men

Till he disbursed at Saint Colme's inch
Ten thousand dollars to our general use.

Enter ROSS

MALCOLM
It's the good lord of Ross

LENNOX
What a hurry he's in, you can almost see it in his eyes!
He looks as if he has something strange and important to say.

ROSS
God save the king!

DUNCAN
Where have you come from good lord?

ROSS
From Fife, great king;
Where the Norwegian banners are flying in the sky like an insult
And frightening our people. The King of Norway himself,
With a huge number of soldiers,
Being helped by that traitor
The Lord of Cawdor, began an ominous battle;
Until Macbeth, wearing heavy armour, as if he were newly-married to Bellona, the Roman Goddess of War,
Fought against him with similar levels of courage and skill.
Disciplining his lack of respect and arrogance: and, to conclude,
We won the battle.

DUNCAN
That's great news!

ROSS
Now
Sweno, the King of Norway, is looking to discuss peace terms:
But we wouldn't even allow him to bury his own men
Until he paid us at Saint Colme's island,
Ten thousand dollars for our use.

DUNCAN No more that thane of Cawdor shall deceive Our bosom interest: go pronounce his present death, And with his former title greet Macbeth. **ROSS** I'll see it done. **DUNCAN** What he hath lost noble Macbeth hath won. *Exeunt*	**DUNCAN** The Lord of Cawdor will no longer trick us in things that are so close to our hearts: go announce he is to be executed, And give his current title to Macbeth. **ROSS** I'll do it now. **DUNCAN** What the Lord of Cawdor has lost, noble Macbeth will gain. *Exeunt*

Act 1 Scene 3

ORIGINAL TEXT	MODERN TRANSLATION
A heath near Forres.	**An open place near Forres.**
Thunder. Enter the three Witches	*Thunder. Enter the three Witches*
First Witch Where hast thou been, sister?	**First Witch** Where have you been sister?
Second Witch Killing swine.	**Second Witch** Killing pigs.
Third Witch Sister, where thou?	**Third Witch** Sister, where were you?
First Witch A sailor's wife had chestnuts in her lap, And munch'd, and munch'd, and munch'd:-- 'Give me,' quoth I: 'Aroint thee, witch!' the rump-fed ronyon cries. Her husband's to Aleppo gone, master o' the Tiger: But in a sieve I'll thither sail, And, like a rat without a tail, I'll do, I'll do, and I'll do.	**First Witch** A sailor's wife had chestnuts in her lap, And ate, and ate and ate: 'Give me them' I said to her: 'Go away, witch!' the fat bottomed lady said. Her husband's gone to Aleppo in Syria, he's the master of the ship The Tiger: But I'll sail in a sieve, And, like a rat without a tail, I'll cause lots of mischief and harm.
Second Witch I'll give thee a wind.	**Second Witch** I'll give you some wind to help cause damage to the ship.
First Witch Thou'rt kind.	**First Witch** You are kind.
Third Witch And I another.	**Third Witch** And I'll give you some wind, too.
First Witch I myself have all the other, And the very ports they blow, All the quarters that they know I' the shipman's card. I will drain him dry as hay: Sleep shall neither night nor day Hang upon his pent-house lid; He shall live a man forbid: Weary se'nnights nine times nine	**First Witch** I control all the other winds, In all the ports where they blow, Every place where they can reach On a sailor's compass. With this wind, I will prevent him from getting to port and taking on fresh water: He won't get any sleep at night or during the day; He will live like a cursed man: For 567 days

Shall he dwindle, peak and pine:
Though his bark cannot be lost,
Yet it shall be tempest-tost.
Look what I have.

Second Witch
Show me, show me.

First Witch
Here I have a pilot's thumb,
Wreck'd as homeward he did come.

Drum within

Third Witch
A drum, a drum!
Macbeth doth come.

ALL
The weird sisters, hand in hand,
Posters of the sea and land,
Thus do go about, about:
Thrice to thine and thrice to mine
And thrice again, to make up nine.
Peace! the charm's wound up.

Enter MACBETH and BANQUO

MACBETH
So foul and fair a day I have not seen.

BANQUO
How far is't call'd to Forres? What are these

So wither'd and so wild in their attire,
That look not like the inhabitants o' the earth,
And yet are on't? Live you? or are you aught
That man may question? You seem to
understand me,
By each at once her chappy finger laying
Upon her skinny lips: you should be women,
And yet your beards forbid me to interpret
That you are so.

MACBETH
Speak, if you can: what are you?

First Witch
All hail, Macbeth! hail to thee, thane of Glamis!

Shall he get thin and miserable:
Although his ship cannot be sunk,
It will experience storms at sea.
Look what I have here.

Second Witch
Show me, show me.

First Witch
Here I have a sailor's thumb
Shipwrecked and drowned as he made his way
home.

Drum within

Third Witch
A drum, a drum!
Macbeth is coming.

ALL
The supernatural sisters, hand in hand,
Fast travellers of the sea and land,
They go around the world:
Three to you and three to me
And three again to make up nine.
Quiet! The spell is ready.

Enter MACBETH and BANQUO

MACBETH
I've not seen a day like this before where the
weather has been so bad but also so good.

BANQUO
How far is it to Forres? What are these things
with clothes so dirty and shabby,
They look like they don't belong here on earth
but yet they are here? Are you alive? Or are
you something that a man might question
whether you are alive or dead? You seem to
understand me,
Looking at your withered finger on
your lips: you should be women,
And yet your beards stop me from
believing that you are.

MACBETH
Speak, if you can: what are you?

First Witch
All hail, Macbeth! Hail to you, Lord of Glamis!

Second Witch

All hail, Macbeth, hail to thee, thane of Cawdor!

Third Witch

All hail, Macbeth, thou shalt be king hereafter!

BANQUO

Good sir, why do you start; and seem to fear
Things that do sound so fair? I' the name of truth,
Are ye fantastical, or that indeed
Which outwardly ye show? My noble partner
You greet with present grace and great prediction
Of noble having and of royal hope,
That he seems rapt withal: to me you speak not.
If you can look into the seeds of time,
And say which grain will grow and which will not,
Speak then to me, who neither beg nor fear
Your favours nor your hate.

First Witch

Hail!

Second Witch

Hail!

Third Witch

Hail!

First Witch

Lesser than Macbeth, and greater.

Second Witch

Not so happy, yet much happier.

Third Witch

Thou shalt get kings, though thou be none:

So all hail, Macbeth and Banquo!

First Witch

Banquo and Macbeth, all hail!

MACBETH

Stay, you imperfect speakers, tell me more:

Second Witch

All hail Macbeth, hail to you, Lord of Cawdor!

Third Witch

All hail Macbeth! You will be king in the future!

BANQUO

Macbeth, why are you so startled;
and afraid of things that sound so good? In the name of truth,
Are you witches imaginary or are you as real as you appear to be?
You greet Macbeth with his present title but also predict
that he will have another noble title and will soon become the king,
He seems completely fascinated by it: You have not said anything to me.
If you can look into the future and say which crops will grow and which will not,
Speak to me about my future, I don't beg for good things from you nor fear bad things.

First Witch

Hail!

Second Witch

Hail!

Third Witch

Hail!

First Witch

You are less than Macbeth, and greater.

Second Witch

Not as happy as him, but much happier.

Third Witch

You shall be the father of kings but not be one yourself:
So all hail, Macbeth and Banquo!

First Witch

Banquo and Macbeth, all hail!

MACBETH

Stay, you incomplete speakers, tell me more:

By Sinel's death I know I am thane of Glamis;	Because Sinel (Macbeth's father) died, I became the Lord of Glamis;
But how of Cawdor? the thane of Cawdor lives,	But how am I Lord of Cawdor? The Lord of Cawdor is alive,
A prosperous gentleman; and to be king Stands not within the prospect of belief, No more than to be Cawdor. Say from whence You owe this strange intelligence? or why Upon this blasted heath you stop our way With such prophetic greeting? Speak, I charge you.	A wealthy gentleman; and that I could be king is something not even worth believing, No more than it it's worth believing I'm the Lord of Cawdor. Tell me from where you got this strange information? Or why, upon this damned field, you stop us on our journey with such a greeting about the future? Speak, I command you.
Witches vanish	*Witches vanish*
BANQUO The earth hath bubbles, as the water has,	**BANQUO** The earth, like the water, has bubbles that spirits
And these are of them. Whither are they vanish'd?	like these can disappear in. Where did they disappear to?
MACBETH Into the air; and what seem'd corporal melted	**MACBETH** Into the air; and what seemed to be made of flesh and blood melted
As breath into the wind. Would they had stay'd!	as if it were breath on the wind. I wish they had stayed!
BANQUO Were such things here as we do speak about?	**BANQUO** Were they even here, these creatures that we're talking about?
Or have we eaten on the insane root That takes the reason prisoner?	Or have we eaten something that has made us go mad?
MACBETH Your children shall be kings.	**MACBETH** Your children shall be kings.
BANQUO You shall be king.	**BANQUO** You shall be king.
MACBETH And thane of Cawdor too: went it not so?	**MACBETH** And Lord of Cawdor too: was that not what they said?
BANQUO To the selfsame tune and words. Who's here?	**BANQUO** Those exact words. Who's coming now?
Enter ROSS and ANGUS	*Enter ROSS and ANGUS*
ROSS The king hath happily received, Macbeth,	**ROSS** The king has happily heard,

Original	Modern
The news of thy success; and when he reads	Macbeth,
	The news of your success in battle; and when he reads
Thy personal venture in the rebels' fight,	About your personal involvement in the fight against the rebels,
His wonders and his praises do contend	He doesn't know whether to praise you or
Which should be thine or his: silenced with that,	express his amazement: Speechless with admiration,
In viewing o'er the rest o' the selfsame day,	He looks through the day's events
He finds thee in the stout Norweyan ranks,	And finds that you also fought against the Norwegians,
Nothing afeard of what thyself didst make,	Unafraid of the hideous and barbaric scene that you created yourself with your killings. Thick and fast
Strange images of death. As thick as hail	Came messengers with messages; and
Came post with post; and every one did bear	everyone was very complimentary
Thy praises in his kingdom's great defence,	about you for defending Scotland and they
And pour'd them down before him.	passed these messages on to the king.
ANGUS	**ANGUS**
We are sent	We have been sent
To give thee from our royal master thanks;	To give you a message of thanks from the King;
Only to herald thee into his sight,	Only this is not the only payment that you will receive.
Not pay thee.	
ROSS	**ROSS**
And, for an earnest of a greater honour,	And, as a token of the honour you are going to receive,
He bade me, from him, call thee thane of Cawdor:	The king told me, from him, to call you lord of Cawdor:
In which addition, hail, most worthy thane!	So, because of this, hail, most worthy lord!
For it is thine.	For it is yours.
BANQUO	**BANQUO**
What, can the devil speak true?	Can these witches have been right?
MACBETH	**MACBETH**
The thane of Cawdor lives: why do you dress me	The Lord of Cawdor is alive: why do you give me another man's title?
In borrow'd robes?	
ANGUS	**ANGUS**
Who was the thane lives yet;	The old Lord of Cawdor is still alive;
But under heavy judgment bears that life	But he won't be for long. There is a case against him
Which he deserves to lose. Whether he was combined	Which he deserves to be killed for. Whether he was helping the Norwegian forces or helped the rebels
With those of Norway, or did line the rebel	By strengthening them and giving them
With hidden help and vantage, or that with both	information or he helped both of them to weaken our country and destroy it,

He labour'd in his country's wreck, I know not;
But treasons capital, confess'd and proved,
Have overthrown him.

MACBETH
[Aside] Glamis, and thane of Cawdor!
The greatest is behind.

To ROSS and ANGUS

Thanks for your pains.

To BANQUO

Do you not hope your children shall be kings,

When those that gave the thane of Cawdor to me
Promised no less to them?

BANQUO
That trusted home
Might yet enkindle you unto the crown,
Besides the thane of Cawdor. But 'tis strange:
And oftentimes, to win us to our harm,
The instruments of darkness tell us truths,
Win us with honest trifles, to betray's
In deepest consequence.

Cousins, a word, I pray you.

MACBETH
[Aside] Two truths are told,
As happy prologues to the swelling act
Of the imperial theme.--I thank you, gentlemen.

This supernatural soliciting
Cannot be ill, cannot be good: if ill,

Why hath it given me earnest of success,
Commencing in a truth? I am thane of Cawdor:
If good, why do I yield to that suggestion

Whose horrid image doth unfix my hair
And make my seated heart knock at my ribs,
Against the use of nature? Present fears
Are less than horrible imaginings:

I do not know;
But he has been destroyed by these treacherous acts which carry the death penalty, to which he has confessed and they've been proved.

MACBETH
[Aside] I'm Lord of Glamis and Lord of Cawdor!
The best is yet to come.

To ROSS and ANGUS

Thanks for all the trouble you've gone to.

To BANQUO

Do you not now hope that your children will be kings,
Because the witches, who have made me Lord of Cawdor
Promised that they would be?

BANQUO
If you accepted that completely it would encourage your hopes of being king as well as Lord of Cawdor. It's strange:
Agents of evil will often tell us simple things that are true so they can
Win us over and make us trust them,
But they will betray us and tell us lies about something much more important.
Friends, can I have a word with you.

MACBETH
[Aside] Two of the witches' prophecies have come true, like two promising introductions to the great story of me becoming king. I thank you gentlemen.
The witches' prophecies
Can't be bad (he will become king), can't be good (Duncan is already king): if bad, why does it promise me great success,
By first making me lord of Cawdor?
If it's a good thing, why do I feel uncomfortable with it
And why do they make my hair stand on end and make my heart beat against my ribs,
In an unnatural way? Frightening things happening now are less terrifying than what we can imagine:

53

My thought, whose murder yet is but fantastical,
Shakes so my single state of man that function
Is smother'd in surmise, and nothing is
But what is not.

BANQUO
Look, how our partner's rapt.

MACBETH
[Aside] If chance will have me king, why, chance may crown me,
Without my stir.

BANQUO
New horrors come upon him,
Like our strange garments, cleave not to their mould
But with the aid of use.

MACBETH
[Aside] Come what come may,
Time and the hour runs through the roughest day.

BANQUO
Worthy Macbeth, we stay upon your leisure.

MACBETH
Give me your favour: my dull brain was wrought
With things forgotten. Kind gentlemen, your pains
Are register'd where every day I turn
The leaf to read them. Let us toward the king.
Think upon what hath chanced, and, at more time,
The interim having weigh'd it, let us speak
Our free hearts each to other.

BANQUO
Very gladly.

MACBETH
Till then, enough. Come, friends.

Exeunt

My mind, which thinks of murder as a fantasy at the moment,
Is shaking me to my core so that I can't do anything except think about the future, and noting is real to me except the fantasy of being king.

BANQUO
Look, how Macbeth is lost in his own thoughts.

MACBETH
[*Aside*] If fate will make me king,
then, I may become king without having to do anything.

BANQUO
His new title does not fit him yet,
Like new clothes that don't fit properly but that we get used to over time.

MACBETH
[*Aside*] Whatever happens will happen,
Even the worst days come to an end.

BANQUO
Good Macbeth, we are ready to go if it suits you.

MACBETH
My apologies: my brain was
taken over
by memories of old. Kind gentlemen,
I will remember
All you have done and I will think about them every day. Let us go to the king.
We should think about what has happened,
and, once we've had time to do that,
We can speak openly about it.

BANQUO
I'd be glad to.

MACBETH
Until then, we've said enough. Come, friends.

Exeunt

Act 1 Scene 4

ORIGINAL TEXT	MODERN TRANSLATION
Forres. The palace.	**Forres. The Palace.**
Flourish. Enter DUNCAN, MALCOLM, DONALBAIN, LENNOX, and Attendants	*Fanfare. Enter DUNCAN, MALCOLM, DONALBAIN, LENNOX and Attendants*
DUNCAN Is execution done on Cawdor? Are not Those in commission yet return'd?	**DUNCAN** Has Cawdor been executed yet? Are the ones who did it not back yet?
MALCOLM My liege, They are not yet come back. But I have spoke With one that saw him die: who did report That very frankly he confess'd his treasons, Implored your highness' pardon and set forth A deep repentance: nothing in his life Became him like the leaving it; he died As one that had been studied in his death To throw away the dearest thing he owed, As 'twere a careless trifle.	**MALCOLM** My lord, They have not come back yet. But I Spoke With someone who saw him die: who told me That he openly confessed to what he had done, Begged for the king to forgive him And displayed A sincere regret: he did nothing in his life to show how noble he was except the way he died. He gave in to death and threw away his life (the dearest thing he owned), As if it were nothing.
DUNCAN There's no art To find the mind's construction in the face: He was a gentleman on whom I built An absolute trust.	**DUNCAN** There's no way Of knowing what someone is thinking By looking at their face: He was someone in whom I put all my trust.
Enter MACBETH, BANQUO, ROSS, and ANGUS O worthiest cousin! The sin of my ingratitude even now Was heavy on me: thou art so far before That swiftest wing of recompense is slow To overtake thee. Would thou hadst less deserved, That the proportion both of thanks and payment Might have been mine! only I have left to say, More is thy due than more than all can pay.	*Enter MACBETH, BANQUO, ROSS and ANGUS* [*To Macbeth*] Oh my good friend! I feel bad that I cannot do enough to show you how grateful I am: you deserve so much more Than payment for what you have done for me. I almost wish that you had done less so that my reward Would be more suited to you. All I can say is that you deserve more than I can ever give you.

MACBETH

The service and the loyalty I owe,
In doing it, pays itself. Your highness' part
Is to receive our duties; and our duties
Are to your throne and state children and servants,
Which do but what they should, by doing every thing
Safe toward your love and honour.

DUNCAN

Welcome hither:
I have begun to plant thee, and will labour
To make thee full of growing. Noble Banquo,

That hast no less deserved, nor must be known
No less to have done so, let me enfold thee
And hold thee to my heart.

BANQUO

There if I grow,
The harvest is your own.

DUNCAN

My plenteous joys,
Wanton in fulness, seek to hide themselves
In drops of sorrow. Sons, kinsmen, thanes,

And you whose places are the nearest, know
We will establish our estate upon
Our eldest, Malcolm, whom we name hereafter
The Prince of Cumberland; which honour must

Not unaccompanied invest him only,

But signs of nobleness, like stars, shall shine
On all deservers. From hence to Inverness,
And bind us further to you.

MACBETH

The rest is labour, which is not used for you:
I'll be myself the harbinger and make joyful

The hearing of my wife with your approach;
So humbly take my leave.

DUNCAN

My worthy Cawdor!

MACBETH

The service and loyalty that I owe to you as my king, is reward enough. Your highness' job
Is to let us be loyal to you: and our duty is to protect the throne and Scotland, we are like children or servants, we only do what we are supposed to do and everything is done for your love and honour.

DUNCAN

Welcome here:
I have tried to grow you like a tree, and I will continue to work to make you great. Noble Banquo,
You deserve no less and it must not be thought That you have done less (in battle) so, let me embrace you and hold you close to my heart.

BANQUO

So if I grow (as you have planted me), then what comes of me belongs to you.

DUNCAN

I'm so happy that I'm shedding tears and trying to hide them. Sons, friends, lords,
And those of you are near to me and in line for the throne,
Know
We will settle the matter of who will become king after me by naming my eldest son, Malcolm, who will be known as The Prince of Cumberland; but he will not be the only one to receive honours,
But everyone who deserves it, will receive them.
From here we shall go to Inverness (Macbeth's castle) and we will be in further debt to you for hosting us.

MACBETH

Anything that is not done for you is hard work:
I'll go ahead as messenger to my home
And make my wife happy
With the news that you are coming;
So I will go now.

DUNCAN

Goodbye, Lord of Cawdor!

MACBETH	**MACBETH**
[Aside] The Prince of Cumberland! that is a step	[*Aside*] Malcolm is the Prince of Cumberland! I will either have to step over (murder) him or I will fail to become king
On which I must fall down, or else o'erleap,	
For in my way it lies. Stars, hide your fires;	Because he stands in my way. Stars, don't shine so brightly;
Let not light see my black and deep desires:	I don't want anyone to see my black and deep desires (to be king):
The eye wink at the hand; yet let that be,	Let my eyes stay closed and not see what my hand is doing: but let my hand do something
Which the eye fears, when it is done, to see.	that, when I've done it, my eyes would be afraid to look at.
Exit	*Exit*
DUNCAN	**DUNCAN**
True, worthy Banquo; he is full so valiant,	Truly, good Banquo; he (Macbeth) is such a courageous person,
And in his commendations I am fed;	And I'm happy to be rewarding him;
It is a banquet to me. Let's after him,	It makes me happy and satisfied. Let's follow
Whose care is gone before to bid us welcome:	him to Inverness where he has gone to prepare a welcome for us:
It is a peerless kinsman.	He is a friend without an equal.
Flourish. Exeunt	*Fanfare. Exit*

ORIGINAL TEXT	MODERN TRANSLATION
Inverness. Macbeth's castle.	**Inverness. Macbeth's castle.**
Enter LADY MACBETH, reading a letter	*Enter LADY MACBETH, reading a letter*
LADY MACBETH	**LADY MACBETH**
'They met me in the day of success: and I have learned by the perfectest report, they have more in them than mortal knowledge. When I burned in desire to question them further, they made themselves air, into which they vanished. Whiles I stood rapt in the wonder of it, came missives from the king, who all-hailed me 'Thane of Cawdor;' by which title, before, these weird sisters saluted me, and referred me to the coming on of time, with 'Hail, king that shalt be!' This have I thought good to deliver thee, my dearest partner of greatness, that thou mightst not lose the dues of rejoicing, by being ignorant of what greatness is promised thee. Lay it to thy heart, and farewell.'	I met them [the witches] after I had helped to win the battle and I learned that they know more than ordinary people do. When I tried to find out more from them, they disappeared into thin air. I was standing there confused when some messengers from the king arrived and they called me Lord of Cawdor just as the witches had, and the witches also called me the future king. I thought it would be good to let you know this news, my dear partner in greatness, so that you too have a chance to celebrate. Keep this news secret and goodbye.
Glamis thou art, and Cawdor; and shalt be What thou art promised: yet do I fear thy nature; It is too full o' the milk of human kindness To catch the nearest way: thou wouldst be great; Art not without ambition, but without The illness should attend it: what thou wouldst highly, That wouldst thou holily; wouldst not play false, And yet wouldst wrongly win: thou'ldst have, great Glamis, That which cries 'Thus thou must do, if thou have it; And that which rather thou dost fear to do Than wishest should be undone.' Hie thee hither, That I may pour my spirits in thine ear; And chastise with the valour of my tongue All that impedes thee from the golden round, Which fate and metaphysical aid doth seem To have thee crown'd withal.	You are already Lord of Glamis and Lord of Cawdor; and you should get what you are promised: But I'm doubtful of your personality; You are too kind to be able to take advantage of opportunities that are before you: You want to be powerful and you do have some ambition, but I don't think you have that mean streak that you need to go with it: what you want to do; you want to do as a good person; you wouldn't cheat, But you still want something that's wrong; these things you want, you want someone else to do for you. You're afraid of what you have to do to get it yourself. Hurry home so I can talk to you and persuade you and get rid of whatever it is that's stopping you from going for the crown, which both fate and the supernatural want you to have.
Enter a Messenger	*Enter a Messenger*
What is your tidings?	What news have you?
Messenger	**Messenger**

The king comes here to-night.

LADY MACBETH
Thou'rt mad to say it:
Is not thy master with him? who, were't so,
Would have inform'd for preparation.

Messenger
So please you, it is true: our thane is coming:
One of my fellows had the speed of him,
Who, almost dead for breath, had scarcely more
Than would make up his message.

LADY MACBETH
Give him tending;
He brings great news.

Exit Messenger

The raven himself is hoarse
That croaks the fatal entrance of Duncan
Under my battlements. Come, you spirits
That tend on mortal thoughts, unsex me here,
And fill me from the crown to the toe top-full
Of direst cruelty! make thick my blood;
Stop up the access and passage to remorse,

That no compunctious visitings of nature
Shake my fell purpose, nor keep peace between

The effect and it! Come to my woman's breasts,
And take my milk for gall, you murdering ministers,
Wherever in your sightless substances
You wait on nature's mischief! Come, thick night,
And pall thee in the dunnest smoke of hell,
That my keen knife see not the wound it makes,
Nor heaven peep through the blanket of the dark,
To cry 'Hold, hold!'

Enter MACBETH

Great Glamis! worthy Cawdor!
Greater than both, by the all-hail hereafter!
Thy letters have transported me beyond
This ignorant present, and I feel now
The future in the instant.

The king is coming to stay here tonight.

LADY MACBETH
You are mad to say that:
Is Macbeth not with him? If this was true,
Macbeth would have told me in advance
so I could get ready.

Messenger
It is true, Macbeth is coming: He sent a
messenger ahead of him to inform you
and he has just arrived, so out of breath
that he hardly had enough air in his lungs
to tell us his message.

LADY MACBETH
Look after him;
He brings great news.

Exit Messenger

The raven [a messenger of death] is hoarse
like this messenger who has arrived to tell
us that Duncan is coming to our castle.
Come, you spirits that encourage thoughts
of murder, change me from a woman to a
man and fill me up from head to toe full of
terrible cruelty! Make my blood thick so
that it clogs up my veins and stops me
from feeling remorse or sorrow,
That no guilty feelings shall stop me from
accomplishing what it is I'm setting out to
do.
Come to my breasts, spirits, and turn my
milk into acid, you murdering spirits
wherever it is that you hide waiting to do
bad things.
Come night time so that you can cover us
in the thickest smoke of hell, so that my
knife won't be able to see the wound that
it makes and heaven won't be able to look
down through the darkness and shout
stop, stop!

Enter MACBETH

Great Glamis, worthy Cawdor!
Soon you'll be greater than both those
titles by what's to come after [becoming
king]! The letter you sent has transported

MACBETH
My dearest love,
Duncan comes here to-night.

LADY MACBETH
And when goes hence?

MACBETH
To-morrow, as he purposes.

LADY MACBETH
O, never
Shall sun that morrow see!
Your face, my thane, is as a book where men

May read strange matters. To beguile the time,
Look like the time; bear welcome in your eye,
Your hand, your tongue: look like the innocent
flower,

But be the serpent under't. He that's coming
Must be provided for: and you shall put
This night's great business into my dispatch;
Which shall to all our nights and days to come
Give solely sovereign sway and masterdom.

MACBETH
We will speak further.

LADY MACBETH
Only look up clear;
To alter favour ever is to fear:
Leave all the rest to me.

Exeunt

me from what's happening now to what's
going to happen in the future.

MACBETH
My dearest Love,
Duncan is coming here tonight.

LADY MACBETH
And when is he leaving?

MACBETH
He intends to leave tomorrow.

LADY MACBETH
O, never will that day come!
Your face, my lord, is as easy to read as a
book where anyone can see what you're
thinking.
To trick people, you must look just as they
would expect. Pretend to welcome the
king with your eyes, your hands and your
voice: look like someone who is innocent
as a flower but be the snake that hides
underneath the flower.
The king must be taken care of this
evening and you should leave everything
to me because what happens tonight will
give us power and control for the rest of
our days.

MACBETH
We will talk about this further.

LADY MACBETH
You need to look like nothing is bothering
you because you can't arouse any
suspicion: leave the rest to me.

Exeunt

ORIGINAL TEXT	MODERN TRANSLATION
Before Macbeth's castle.	**Before Macbeth's castle.**
Hautboys and torches. Enter DUNCAN, MALCOLM, DONALBAIN, BANQUO, LENNOX, MACDUFF, ROSS, ANGUS, and Attendants	*Boys playing large wooden instruments and bearing torches. Enter DUNCAN, MALCOLM, DONALBAIN, BANQUO, LENNOX, MACDUFF, ROSS, ANGUS and Attendants.*
DUNCAN This castle hath a pleasant seat; the air Nimbly and sweetly recommends itself Unto our gentle senses.	**DUNCAN** This castle is in a pleasant place; the air is nice and sweet and is pleasing to our senses.
BANQUO This guest of summer, The temple-haunting martlet, does approve, By his loved mansionry, that the heaven's breath Smells wooingly here: no jutty, frieze, Buttress, nor coign of vantage, but this bird Hath made his pendent bed and procreant cradle: Where they most breed and haunt, I have observed, The air is delicate.	**BANQUO** This bird of the summer, the house martin, approves of this place and has built his nest here which shows how sweet the air is. No part of the castle walls is without house martin nests, where they sleep and breed: they choose places where the air is best for their nests so it is a great compliment to Macbeths' castle.
Enter LADY MACBETH	*Enter LADY MACBETH*
DUNCAN See, see, our honour'd hostess! The love that follows us sometime is our trouble, Which still we thank as love. Herein I teach you How you shall bid God 'ild us for your pains, And thank us for your trouble.	**DUNCAN** Look, here comes our honourable hostess! The love that comes from our subjects is sometimes an annoyance, But we still have to be thankful for it. From here, I teach you to look upon our visit, although, troublesome to you, as something good and that you may thank us for putting you to this trouble.
LADY MACBETH All our service In every point twice done and then done double Were poor and single business to contend Against those honours deep and broad wherewith Your majesty loads our house: for those of old, And the late dignities heap'd up to them, We rest your hermits.	**LADY MACBETH** Everything we do, even if we had to do it twice and then twice over again, were nothing compared to the honour you have done us by coming here and staying with us and also the new honours that you've bestowed upon us. Welcome, and rest.

DUNCAN
Where's the thane of Cawdor?
We coursed him at the heels, and had a purpose
To be his purveyor: but he rides well;
And his great love, sharp as his spur, hath holp him
To his home before us. Fair and noble hostess,

We are your guest to-night.

LADY MACBETH
Your servants ever
Have theirs, themselves and what is theirs, in compt,
To make their audit at your highness' pleasure,
Still to return your own.

DUNCAN
Give me your hand;
Conduct me to mine host: we love him highly,
And shall continue our graces towards him.

By your leave, hostess.

Exeunt

DUNCAN
Where's the Lord of Cawdor?
We followed him closely and had hoped to
get here before him: but he rides fast and
his great love [Lady Macbeth] had acted as
encouragement to help him ride faster and
get here before us. Fair and noble hostess,
We are your guests tonight.

LADY MACBETH
As ever, we are your servants and what is
ours is also yours because you are the
reason that we have it and it's only right to
give back to you.

DUNCAN
Give me your hand;
Bring me to my host: we think an awful lot
of him, and will continue to think highly of
him.
We're waiting for you, hostess.

Exeunt

Act 1 Scene 7

ORIGINAL TEXT	MODERN TEXT
SCENE VII. Macbeth's castle.	**SCENE 7 Macbeth's castle.**
Hautboys and torches. Enter a Sewer, and divers Servants with dishes and service, and pass over the stage. Then enter MACBETH	*Boys playing large wooden instruments and bearing torches. Enter a lead servant followed by lots of other servants carrying dishes, food, and utensils. Enter MACBETH*
MACBETH	**MACBETH**
If it were done when 'tis done, then 'twere well It were done quickly: if the assassination Could trammel up the consequence, and catch With his surcease success; that but this blow Might be the be-all and the end-all here, But here, upon this bank and shoal of time, We'd jump the life to come. But in these cases We still have judgment here; that we but teach Bloody instructions, which, being taught, return To plague the inventor: this even-handed justice Commends the ingredients of our poison'd chalice To our own lips. He's here in double trust; First, as I am his kinsman and his subject, Strong both against the deed; then, as his host, Who should against his murderer shut the door, Not bear the knife myself. Besides, this Duncan Hath borne his faculties so meek, hath been So clear in his great office, that his virtues Will plead like angels, trumpet-tongued, against The deep damnation of his taking-off; And pity, like a naked new-born babe, Striding the blast, or heaven's cherubim, horsed Upon the sightless couriers of the air, Shall blow the horrid deed in every eye, That tears shall drown the wind. I have no spur To prick the sides of my intent, but only Vaulting ambition, which o'erleaps itself And falls on the other.	If it's going to be done and finished: if everything could be finished and done with after murder and there were no consequences and that was the end of it then murder would be the be-all and end-all of the whole thing and I'd gladly do the deed and put my soul at risk for the rewards I'd get here. But if we commit murder, we still have to face judgement here, by doing it, we teach other people to do it and, eventually, these teachings will return to haunt the teacher: Justice is even-handed so that what we do to others, must be done to ourselves. Duncan trusts me in two ways; firstly, I'm his friend and his subject so my first duty is to always protect him. Secondly, I'm his host so I should be protecting him against anyone who would want to murder him, not trying to murder him myself. Besides this, Duncan has been such a good and innocent leader that all these good things will be what people remember of him when he's dead and they will play like angels playing trumpets against the terrible sin of his murder. And pity, like a naked new-born child, will take flight on the wind and tell everyone of the terrible deed that has taken place and they will all know and they will all shed so many tears that it will be like a flood trying to drown the wind. There is nothing that can encourage me to do this except my ambition, which goes ahead of myself and brings me close to disaster.
Enter LADY MACBETH	*Enter LADY MACBETH*
How now! what news?	How are things? What's the news?

LADY MACBETH

He has almost supp'd: why have you left the chamber?

MACBETH

Hath he ask'd for me?

LADY MACBETH

Know you not he has?

MACBETH

We will proceed no further in this business:
He hath honour'd me of late; and I have bought
Golden opinions from all sorts of people,
Which would be worn now in their newest gloss,
Not cast aside so soon.

LADY MACBETH

Was the hope drunk
Wherein you dress'd yourself? hath it slept since?
And wakes it now, to look so green and pale
At what it did so freely? From this time
Such I account thy love. Art thou afeard
To be the same in thine own act and valour
As thou art in desire? Wouldst thou have that
Which thou esteem'st the ornament of life,
And live a coward in thine own esteem,
Letting 'I dare not' wait upon 'I would,'
Like the poor cat i' the adage?

MACBETH

Prithee, peace:
I dare do all that may become a man;
Who dares do more is none.

LADY MACBETH

What beast was't, then,
That made you break this enterprise to me?
When you durst do it, then you were a man;
And, to be more than what you were, you would
Be so much more the man. Nor time nor place
Did then adhere, and yet you would make both:
They have made themselves, and that their fitness now
Does unmake you. I have given suck, and know
How tender 'tis to love the babe that milks me:
I would, while it was smiling in my face,

LADY MACBETH

He has almost finished eating: why have you left the room?

MACBETH

Did he ask for me?

LADY MACBETH

Don't you know that he has?

MACBETH

We can't go any further with this plan:
He has given me lots of honours lately and I have gained the respect and good opinions of lots of people. I should be enjoying all this new attention and respect, not throwing it away.

LADY MACBETH

Were you drunk when we were speaking about this before? Have you fallen asleep and woken up all green and pale and afraid at what we planned before?
From here on out, this is what I will think of your love. Are you so afraid to get what you want? Will you try to become king, the thing you want so badly, or will you live as a coward, always saying 'I dare not' after you say 'I want' something, like the cat in that old story?

MACBETH

Please, stop: I'm willing to do everything that I can to become a man; whoever is willing to do more is not a man.

LADY MACBETH

What beast was it then that first thought of doing this? When you planned to do this, that's when you were a real man;
And, if you do it, then you'll be even more a man. When you thought of it before, the time and place weren't right but now both are right but the perfectness of it all is stopping you from doing it.
I have breast-fed a child and I know how tender it is to love that child that drinks my milk but I would, while the child was smiling in my face, have taken my nipple from its toothless mouth

64

Have pluck'd my nipple from his boneless gums,
And dash'd the brains out, had I so sworn as you
Have done to this.

MACBETH
If we should fail?

LADY MACBETH
We fail!
But screw your courage to the sticking-place,
And we'll not fail. When Duncan is asleep--
Whereto the rather shall his day's hard journey
Soundly invite him--his two chamberlains
Will I with wine and wassail so convince
That memory, the warder of the brain,
Shall be a fume, and the receipt of reason
A limbeck only: when in swinish sleep
Their drenched natures lie as in a death,
What cannot you and I perform upon
The unguarded Duncan? what not put upon
His spongy officers, who shall bear the guilt
Of our great quell?

MACBETH
Bring forth men-children only;
For thy undaunted mettle should compose
Nothing but males. Will it not be received,
When we have mark'd with blood those sleepy two
Of his own chamber and used their very daggers,
That they have done't?

LADY MACBETH
Who dares receive it other,
As we shall make our griefs and clamour roar
Upon his death?

MACBETH
I am settled, and bend up
Each corporal agent to this terrible feat.
Away, and mock the time with fairest show:
False face must hide what the false heart doth know.

Exeunt

---

and smashed its brains out on the floor if I had sworn to do it, just like you've sworn to do this.

MACBETH
What if we fail?

LADY MACBETH
We fail!
But tighten up your courage and we won't fail. When Duncan is asleep – all his travelling has made him tired – I will get his two servants so drunk that their memories will disappear as if they were gases escaping from their brains. Then, when they're sleeping like pigs, it will be as if they are dead to the world. Then you and I can do whatever we like to the sleeping Duncan and blame it on his servants, who will bear the guilt of our great murder.

MACBETH
I hope that you only ever have sons because your spirit and personality should create nothing but males.
Will people really think, when we have smeared Duncan's servants with his blood and used their very own daggers that they really did it?

LADY MACBETH
Who would think otherwise? We will make our grief at his death known once we've heard the news.

MACBETH
I have decided to do it. I will do everything I can to commit this terrible crime. Go now and pretend to be an honourable hostess and hide with a friendly face, the evil plan in your heart.

Exeunt

Act 2 Scene 1

ORIGINAL TEXT	MODERN TRANSLATION
Court of Macbeth's castle.	**Court of Macbeth's castle**
Enter BANQUO, and FLEANCE bearing a torch before him	*Enter BANQUO, and FLEANCE carrying a torch*
BANQUO How goes the night, boy?	**BANQUO** How is the night going, boy?
FLEANCE The moon is down; I have not heard the clock.	**FLEANCE** The moon has set; but I don't know what time it is.
BANQUO And she goes down at twelve.	**BANQUO** The moon usually sets at midnight.
FLEANCE I take't, 'tis later, sir.	**FLEANCE** If that's the case, then it must be later than midnight, sir.
BANQUO Hold, take my sword. There's husbandry in heaven; Their candles are all out. Take thee that too. A heavy summons lies like lead upon me, And yet I would not sleep: merciful powers, Restrain in me the cursed thoughts that nature Gives way to in repose!	**BANQUO** Here, take my sword. There must be good housekeeping in heaven because they are saving their candles [stars]. Take this too, I'm tired and weary and yet I must not sleep: merciful powers, keep me from having the terrible nightmares that come when I rest.
Enter MACBETH, and a Servant with a torch	*Enter MACBETH and a Servant with a torch*
Give me my sword. Who's there?	Give me my sword. Who's there?
MACBETH A friend.	**MACBETH** A friend.
BANQUO What, sir, not yet at rest? The king's a-bed: He hath been in unusual pleasure, and Sent forth great largess to your offices. This diamond he greets your wife withal, By the name of most kind hostess; and shut up In measureless content.	**BANQUO** What's this, sir, have you not gone to bed yet? The king has: He was in an unusually good mood and has sent forth great gifts to your household. He has given this diamond to your wife for being such a kind and attentive hostess and gone to bed a happy man.

MACBETH
Being unprepared,
Our will became the servant to defect;
Which else should free have wrought.

BANQUO
All's well.
I dreamt last night of the three weird sisters:
To you they have show'd some truth.

MACBETH
I think not of them:
Yet, when we can entreat an hour to serve,
We would spend it in some words upon that business,
If you would grant the time.

BANQUO
At your kind'st leisure.

MACBETH
If you shall cleave to my consent, when 'tis,
It shall make honour for you.

BANQUO
So I lose none
In seeking to augment it, but still keep
My bosom franchised and allegiance clear,
I shall be counsell'd.

MACBETH
Good repose the while!

BANQUO
Thanks, sir: the like to you!

Exeunt BANQUO and FLEANCE

MACBETH
Go bid thy mistress, when my drink is ready,
She strike upon the bell. Get thee to bed.

Exit Servant

Is this a dagger which I see before me,
The handle toward my hand? Come, let me clutch thee.
I have thee not, and yet I see thee still.
Art thou not, fatal vision, sensible
To feeling as to sight? or art thou but

MACBETH
Because we were unprepared for his visit, we were unable to be as generous to the king as we would have otherwise liked.

BANQUO
Everything is good. I had a dream last night about the three witches: They have been truthful about you.

MACBETH
I don't think about them:
Yet, when the time comes, we can talk for an hour or so about them if you would like.

BANQUO
Whenever suits you.

MACBETH
If you shall stay loyal to me, when the time comes, it will bring you honours.

BANQUO
So long as I don't lose any honour by trying to add more, but still keep myself in clear conscience and loyal to my king then I will do whatever you say.

MACBETH
Good, rest now for a while.

BANQUO
Thanks sir, the same to you

Exeunt BANQUO and FLEANCE

MACBETH
Go and tell Lady Macbeth that when my drink is ready, to strike the bell. Then go to bed.

Exit Servant

Is this a dagger that I see in front of me,
Its handle pointing towards my hand? Let me try to grab it [he grabs]. I don't have the dagger but I can still see it.
Am I unable to touch you even though I can see you? Or are you something that I've created in

A dagger of the mind, a false creation,
Proceeding from the heat-oppressed brain?

I see thee yet, in form as palpable
As this which now I draw.
Thou marshall'st me the way that I was going;

And such an instrument I was to use.
Mine eyes are made the fools o' the other
senses,
Or else worth all the rest; I see thee still,
And on thy blade and dudgeon gouts of blood,
Which was not so before. There's no such thing:
It is the bloody business which informs
Thus to mine eyes. Now o'er the one halfworld
Nature seems dead, and wicked dreams abuse
The curtain'd sleep; witchcraft celebrates
Pale Hecate's offerings, and wither'd murder,
Alarum'd by his sentinel, the wolf,
Whose howl's his watch, thus with his stealthy
pace.
With Tarquin's ravishing strides, towards his
design
Moves like a ghost. Thou sure and firm-set
earth,
Hear not my steps, which way they walk, for
fear
Thy very stones prate of my whereabout,
And take the present horror from the time,
Which now suits with it. Whiles I threat, he
lives:
Words to the heat of deeds too cold breath
gives.

A bell rings

I go, and it is done; the bell invites me.
Hear it not, Duncan; for it is a knell
That summons thee to heaven or to hell.

Exit

my mind, a hallucination, that has come from
my overactive imagination?
I can still see you, and you seem as real as this
other dagger [he takes out his own dagger].
You are leading me the way that I was already
going:
And I was going to use a dagger too!
My eyes are either being tricked by all my other
senses or they are better than all the rest of
them put together; I can still see this dagger
and on the blade, thick drops of blood which
were not there before.
There's no such thing:
It is our current blood-fuelled plans [to murder
Duncan] which makes me see this vision. Now,
half the world is asleep and evil dreams keep
people from sleeping properly: people who
practise witchcraft everywhere are giving up
offerings to their god, Hecate, and the old man
of murder, called by his guard the wolf, creeps
quickly like Tarquin [a Roman prince who crept
into a woman's bedroom to rape her] towards
his goal.
You, solid and firm ground, do not hear which
way my steps go because I don't want their
sound to echo back and let people know my
whereabouts and break this silence which suits
the deed I'm about to do. While I talk about
this, Duncan is still alive: The more words I use,
the more my courage is beginning to go cold.

A bell rings

That bell is telling me to go, it is done.
Don't listen to that bell, Duncan because its
ringing means you are either going to heaven
or hell.

Exit

ORIGINAL TEXT	MODERN TRANSLATION
The same.	**The same.**
Enter LADY MACBETH	*Enter LADY MACBETH*
LADY MACBETH That which hath made them drunk hath made me bold; What hath quench'd them hath given me fire. Hark! Peace! It was the owl that shriek'd, the fatal bellman, Which gives the stern'st good-night. He is about it: The doors are open; and the surfeited grooms Do mock their charge with snores: I have drugg'd their possets, That death and nature do contend about them, Whether they live or die.	**LADY MACBETH** The alcohol that I used to get the guards drunk has lifted my courage; That which made them lifeless and asleep, has given me courage and desire to do the deed. Quiet! Listen! It was the owl that shrieked like the man who rings the bell before someone is executed. Macbeth is doing it: The doors are open and the servants, who have drank so much, are mocking their duty by being asleep: I have drugged their drinks so that nobody can tell even if they are alive or dead.
MACBETH [Within] Who's there? what, ho!	**MACBETH** [*offstage*] Who's there? What is it?
LADY MACBETH Alack, I am afraid they have awaked, And 'tis not done. The attempt and not the deed Confounds us. Hark! I laid their daggers ready; He could not miss 'em. Had he not resembled My father as he slept, I had done't.	**LADY MACBETH** Oh no! I'm afraid that they have woken up and the murder hasn't been completed. It is the attempted murder and not the murder itself that will get us in trouble. What's that noise? I put the servants' daggers where Macbeth could not miss them. If Duncan hadn't looked like my father while he was sleeping, I would have done it myself.
Enter MACBETH	*Enter MACBETH*
My husband!	My husband!
MACBETH I have done the deed. Didst thou not hear a noise?	**MACBETH** I have murdered him. Did you hear that noise?
LADY MACBETH I heard the owl scream and the crickets cry. Did not you speak?	**LADY MACBETH** I heard an owl shriek and I heard crickets chirping. Did you not say something?
MACBETH	**MACBETH**

When?

LADY MACBETH
Now.

MACBETH
As I descended?

LADY MACBETH
Ay.

MACBETH
Hark!
Who lies i' the second chamber?

LADY MACBETH
Donalbain.

MACBETH
This is a sorry sight.

Looking on his hands

LADY MACBETH
A foolish thought, to say a sorry sight.

MACBETH
There's one did laugh in's sleep, and one cried 'Murder!'
That they did wake each other: I stood and heard them:
But they did say their prayers, and address'd them
Again to sleep.

LADY MACBETH
There are two lodged together.

MACBETH
One cried 'God bless us!' and 'Amen' the other;
As they had seen me with these hangman's hands.
Listening their fear, I could not say 'Amen,'
When they did say 'God bless us!'

LADY MACBETH
Consider it not so deeply.

MACBETH
But wherefore could not I pronounce 'Amen'?

When?

LADY MACBETH
Just now.

MACBETH
As I was coming down?

LADY MACBETH
Yes.

MACBETH
Listen!
Who is sleeping in the second room?

LADY MACBETH
Donalbain [Duncan's son].

MACBETH
This is a sorry sight.

Looking on his hands

LADY MACBETH
You're being silly to say it's a sorry sight.

MACBETH
One of the servants laughed in his sleep and another one cried out 'Murder!'
That woke the other one: I stood and listened to them: but they just said their prayers and went back to sleep.

LADY MACBETH
There are two people in the same room [Malcolm and Donalbain].

MACBETH
One cried 'God bless us!' and the other said 'Amen';
As though they had seen me murdering Duncan. Listening to their fear, I was unable to say 'Amen' when he said 'God bless us!'

LADY MACBETH
Don't think about it so much.

MACBETH
But why couldn't I say 'Amen'?

I had most need of blessing, and 'Amen'
Stuck in my throat.

LADY MACBETH
These deeds must not be thought
After these ways; so, it will make us mad.

MACBETH
Methought I heard a voice cry 'Sleep no more!
Macbeth does murder sleep', the innocent sleep,
Sleep that knits up the ravell'd sleeve of care,
The death of each day's life, sore labour's bath,
Balm of hurt minds, great nature's second course,
Chief nourisher in life's feast,--

LADY MACBETH
What do you mean?

MACBETH
Still it cried 'Sleep no more!' to all the house:
'Glamis hath murder'd sleep, and therefore Cawdor
Shall sleep no more; Macbeth shall sleep no more.'

LADY MACBETH
Who was it that thus cried? Why, worthy thane,
You do unbend your noble strength, to think
So brainsickly of things. Go get some water,
And wash this filthy witness from your hand.

Why did you bring these daggers from the place?
They must lie there: go carry them; and smear
The sleepy grooms with blood.

MACBETH
I'll go no more:
I am afraid to think what I have done;
Look on't again I dare not.

LADY MACBETH
Infirm of purpose!
Give me the daggers: the sleeping and the dead
Are but as pictures: 'tis the eye of childhood
That fears a painted devil. If he do bleed,

I really needed a blessing and the word 'Amen'
stuck in my throat, I couldn't say it.

LADY MACBETH
We should not think about what we have done
like this, it will make us go mad.

MACBETH
I thought I heard a voice saying 'Sleep no more!
Macbeth has murdered sleep', the innocent
sleep that helps us get our thoughts together,
the sleep we go to at the end of each day, the
sleep that soothes tired workers and hurt
minds, Sleep, the main part of life's great feast
and the most nourishing.

LADY MACBETH
What do you mean by all this?

MACBETH
Still the voice cried 'sleep no more!' all over the
house:
'Glamis has murdered sleep and because of this
Cawdor will no longer be able to sleep;
Macbeth will no longer be able to sleep'.

LADY MACBETH
Who was it that said this? Why, worthy Lord,
you will make yourself weak to think about
these things. Go and get some water, and wash
this blood, that acts like a witness to your
crime, from your hand.
Why did you bring these daggers from the place
of the murder?
They must stay there: go and bring them back;
and smear the sleepy servants with the blood
from them.

MACBETH
No, I won't go back there:
I am afraid to think about what I've done, let
alone look at it.

LADY MACBETH
You weakling!
Give me the daggers then: a dead person looks
just the same as a sleeping person and both
look like pictures: It's only children who are
afraid of these sort of pictures. If Duncan
bleeds,

I'll gild the faces of the grooms withal;

For it must seem their guilt.

Exit. Knocking within

MACBETH
Whence is that knocking?
How is't with me, when every noise appals me?
What hands are here? ha! they pluck out mine eyes.
Will all great Neptune's ocean wash this blood
Clean from my hand? No, this my hand will rather
The multitudinous seas in incarnadine,
Making the green one red.

Re-enter LADY MACBETH

LADY MACBETH
My hands are of your colour; but I shame
To wear a heart so white.

Knocking within

I hear a knocking
At the south entry: retire we to our chamber;
A little water clears us of this deed:
How easy is it, then! Your constancy
Hath left you unattended.

Knocking within

Hark! more knocking.
Get on your nightgown, lest occasion call us,
And show us to be watchers. Be not lost
So poorly in your thoughts.

MACBETH
To know my deed, 'twere best not know myself.

Knocking within

Wake Duncan with thy knocking! I would thou couldst!

Exeunt

I'll cover the faces of the servants with his blood;
It has to look as though they're guilty.

Exit. Knocking within

MACBETH
Where is that knocking coming from?
How is it that every noise I hear frightens me?
Whose hands are these? Ha! They try to pluck out my eyes.
Will all of great Neptune's ocean be able to wash this blood from my hands? No, it's more likely that my hands will turn the massive seas from green to red.

Re-enter LADY MACBETH

LADY MACBETH
My hands are red like yours; but I would be ashamed if my heart were as white as yours [cowardly].

Knocking within

I hear a knocking
At the south door: let's go to our bedroom;
A little water will take the blood off and it will appear like we never did it. How easy is that? You've lost your composure.

Knocking within

Listen! More knocking.
Get your nightgown on in case we're called and people see that we're out of bed. Stop being lost in your thoughts.

MACBETH
Knowing what I've done, I wish I couldn't recognise mysef [because then I wouldn't have to condemn myself].

Knocking within

Wake Duncan with your knocking!
I wish you could!

Exeunt

ORIGINAL TEXT	MODERN TRANSLATION
The same.	**The same.**
Knocking within. Enter a Porter	*Knocking within. Enter a Porter*
Porter Here's a knocking indeed! If a man were porter of hell-gate, he should have old turning the key.	**Porter** This is real knocking here! If a man was the porter of the gates of hell he would have to unlock it many times.
Knocking within	*Knocking within*
Knock, knock, knock! Who's there, i' the name of Beelzebub? Here's a farmer, that hanged himself on the expectation of plenty: come in time; have napkins enow about you; here you'll sweat for't.	Knock, knock, knock! Who's there, in the name of the devil? Maybe it's a farmer who killed himself because the price of grain was so low. You're just in time! I hope you brought some napkins because you're going to sweat a lot in here.
Knocking within	*Knocking within*
Knock, knock! Who's there, in the other devil's name? Faith, here's an equivocator, that could swear in both the scales against either scale; who committed treason enough for God's sake, yet could not equivocate to heaven: O, come in, equivocator.	Knock, knock! Who's there in the other devil's name? Sure enough, here's a two-faced con man who does not tell lies but does not tell the truth and can trick both sides into believing him. He found out, however, that you cannot talk your way into heaven and he committed enough crimes to deserve his place in hell. Come in con man.
Knocking within	*Knocking within*
Knock, knock, knock! Who's there? Faith, here's an English tailor come hither, for stealing out of a French hose: come in, tailor; here you may roast your goose.	Knock, knock, knock! Who's there? Well it's an English tailor coming for trying to trick people by using less fabric than customers paid for but now that French breeches are in fashion, he can't do it anymore; here you may heat your iron.
Knocking within	*Knocking within*
Knock, knock; never at quiet! What are you? But this place is too cold for hell. I'll devil-porter it no further: I had thought to have let in some of all professions that go the primrose way to the everlasting bonfire.	Knock, knock; it's never quiet here! Who is it? Ah, this place is too cold to be hell. I'll no longer pretend to be the devil's porter: I would have let someone from every different profession in the world in.

Knocking within

Anon, anon! I pray you, remember the porter.

Opens the gate

Enter MACDUFF and LENNOX

MACDUFF
Was it so late, friend, ere you went to bed,
That you do lie so late?

Porter
'Faith sir, we were carousing till the
second cock: and drink, sir, is a great
provoker of three things.

MACDUFF
What three things does drink especially
provoke?

Porter
Marry, sir, nose-painting, sleep, and
urine. Lechery, sir, it provokes, and unprovokes;
it provokes the desire, but it takes
away the performance: therefore, much drink
may be said to be an equivocator with lechery:
it makes him, and it mars him; it sets
him on, and it takes him off; it persuades him,
and disheartens him; makes him stand to, and
not stand to; in conclusion, equivocates him
in a sleep, and, giving him the lie, leaves him.

MACDUFF
I believe drink gave thee the lie last night.

Porter
That it did, sir, i' the very throat on
me: but I requited him for his lie; and, I
think, being too strong for him, though he took
up my legs sometime, yet I made a shift to cast
him.

MACDUFF
Is thy master stirring?

Enter MACBETH

Knocking within

Coming, I'm coming! Please remember to tip
the porter.

Opens the gate

Enter MACDUFF and LENNOX

MACDUFF
Is it because you went to bed so late that you
stay in bed this late now?

Porter
It was sir, we were having fun until three
o'clock in the morning: and drink, sir, causes
three things.

MACDUFF
What three things would they be?

Porter
Well sir, it causes your nose to go red, it causes
you to sleep and it causes you to urinate.
Sexual desire, sir, it provokes it and unprovokes
it; It causes the desire but it takes away the
ability to perform: therefore, too much drink
may be said to be a two-faced con man with
sex: it's good for it and bad for it; it sets him up
for it but won't let him do anything about it; it
persuades and disheartens him, it gives you an
erection but then takes it away; in conclusion, it
gives you a dream and then leaves you.

MACDUFF
I bet drink did all this to you last night.

Porter
It did sir, it got right in my throat but I was able
to get the better of drink and I, being too
strong for him, although he made my legs
unsteady at times, I made an effort to vomit
him up.

MACDUFF
Is your master awake?

Enter MACBETH

Our knocking has awaked him; here he comes.	Our knocking has woken him up; here he comes now.
LENNOX Good morrow, noble sir.	**LENNOX** Good morning, noble sir.
MACBETH Good morrow, both.	**MACBETH** Good morning to both of you.
MACDUFF Is the king stirring, worthy thane?	**MACDUFF** Is the king awake, worthy Lord?
MACBETH Not yet.	**MACBETH** Not yet.
MACDUFF He did command me to call timely on him: I have almost slipp'd the hour.	**MACDUFF** He told me to call for him early: I 'm almost late.
MACBETH I'll bring you to him.	**MACBETH** I'll bring you to him.
MACDUFF I know this is a joyful trouble to you; But yet 'tis one.	**MACDUFF** I know having the king here is both an honour but also a lot of work.
MACBETH The labour we delight in physics pain. This is the door.	**MACBETH** Work that we enjoy cures the pain of it. This is the door.
MACDUFF I'll make so bold to call, For 'tis my limited service.	**MACDUFF** I'll wake him, it's my job.
Exit	*Exit*
LENNOX Goes the king hence to-day?	**LENNOX** Is the king leaving here today?
MACBETH He does: he did appoint so.	**MACBETH** He is: he told us to arrange it.
LENNOX The night has been unruly: where we lay, Our chimneys were blown down; and, as they say, Lamentings heard i' the air; strange screams of death, And prophesying with accents terrible Of dire combustion and confused events	**LENNOX** Last night was crazy: the place where we were staying, the chimneys were blown down and people said that they heard strange voices crying on the air; strange screams of death and fortune telling of terrible things that will occur and bring with it a new dreadful era.

New hatch'd to the woeful time: the obscure bird
Clamour'd the livelong night: some say, the earth
Was feverous and did shake.

MACBETH
'Twas a rough night.

LENNOX
My young remembrance cannot parallel
A fellow to it.

Re-enter MACDUFF

MACDUFF
O horror, horror, horror! Tongue nor heart
Cannot conceive nor name thee!

MACBETH LENNOX
What's the matter.

MACDUFF
Confusion now hath made his masterpiece!
Most sacrilegious murder hath broke ope
The Lord's anointed temple, and stole thence
The life o' the building!

MACBETH
What is 't you say? the life?

LENNOX
Mean you his majesty?

MACDUFF
Approach the chamber, and destroy your sight
With a new Gorgon: do not bid me speak;
See, and then speak yourselves.

Exeunt MACBETH and LENNOX

Awake, awake!
Ring the alarum-bell. Murder and treason!
Banquo and Donalbain! Malcolm! awake!
Shake off this downy sleep, death's counterfeit,
And look on death itself! up, up, and see
The great doom's image! Malcolm! Banquo!
As from your graves rise up, and walk like sprites,

The owl shrieked all night long: some people say that the earth was shaking as if it had a fever.

MACBETH
It was a rough night.

LENNOX
I'm of too young an age to remember anything like it.

Re-enter MACDUFF

MACDUFF
Oh horror, horror, horror! This is so terrible that I can't speak it or feel it in my heart!

MACBETH & LENNOX
What's the matter?

MACDUFF
There's been an act of unspeakable destruction!
Someone has broken into the temple blessed by God [the king was believed by the people to be close to God] and taken the life from it.

MACBETH
What are you talking about? What life?

LENNOX
Do you mean the king?

MACDUFF
Go to the room and see the terrible thing for yourselves. Do not ask me questions about it, go and look at it and then you can talk.

Exeunt MACBETH and LENNOX

Wake up, wake up!
Ring the alarm bell! There has been murder and treason!
Banquo and Donalbain! Malcolm! Wake up!
Shake off sleep that is an imitation of death and see death for real! Get up, get up and see this image of the final judgement! Malcolm! Banquo!

To countenance this horror! Ring the bell.

Bell rings

Enter LADY MACBETH

LADY MACBETH
What's the business,
That such a hideous trumpet calls to parley
The sleepers of the house? speak, speak!

MACDUFF
O gentle lady,
'Tis not for you to hear what I can speak:
The repetition, in a woman's ear,
Would murder as it fell.

Enter BANQUO

O Banquo, Banquo,
Our royal master 's murder'd!

LADY MACBETH
Woe, alas!
What, in our house?

BANQUO
Too cruel any where.
Dear Duff, I prithee, contradict thyself,
And say it is not so.

Re-enter MACBETH and LENNOX, with ROSS

MACBETH
Had I but died an hour before this chance,
I had lived a blessed time; for, from this instant,
There 's nothing serious in mortality:
All is but toys: renown and grace is dead;
The wine of life is drawn, and the mere lees
Is left this vault to brag of.

Enter MALCOLM and DONALBAIN

DONALBAIN
What is amiss?

MACBETH
You are, and do not know't:

Get up from your beds like ghosts from their graves and come and this horror! Ring the bell.

Bell ring

Enter LADY MACBETH

LADY MACBETH
What's going on that you have such a terrible ringing to wake up everyone asleep in the house? Speak, speak!

MACDUFF
Oh gentle lady, it's not for your ears, the news I have to say. To tell it to a woman would kill her dead.

Enter BANQUO

Oh Banquo, Banquo, our royal master has been murdered!

LADY MACBETH
Oh, my goodness!
What, in our house?

BANQUO
It is a terrible thing, wherever it happens. My dear Macduff, I beg you, contradict yourself and say that it's not true.

Re-enter MACBETH and LENNOX with ROSS

MACBETH
If only I had died an hour before I heard this news
and I would have lived a truly blessed life. From this instant onwards, there's nothing worth living for, everything is trivial: renown and grace is dead; the wine of life has been poured down the drain and all that's left is the bits at the bottom of the bottle.

Enter MALCOLM and DONALBAIN

DONALBAIN
What's wrong?

MACBETH
You are but you don't know it yet:

The spring, the head, the fountain of your blood
Is stopp'd; the very source of it is stopp'd.

MACDUFF
Your royal father 's murder'd.

MALCOLM
O, by whom?

LENNOX
Those of his chamber, as it seem'd, had done 't:
Their hands and faces were an badged with blood;
So were their daggers, which unwiped we found
Upon their pillows:
They stared, and were distracted; no man's life
Was to be trusted with them.

MACBETH
O, yet I do repent me of my fury,
That I did kill them.

MACDUFF
Wherefore did you so?

MACBETH
Who can be wise, amazed, temperate and furious,
Loyal and neutral, in a moment? No man:
The expedition my violent love
Outrun the pauser, reason. Here lay Duncan,
His silver skin laced with his golden blood;
And his gash'd stabs look'd like a breach in nature
For ruin's wasteful entrance: there, the murderers,
Steep'd in the colours of their trade, their daggers
Unmannerly breech'd with gore: who could refrain,
That had a heart to love, and in that heart
Courage to make 's love kno wn?

LADY MACBETH
Help me hence, ho!

MACDUFF
Look to the lady.

The source of your blood has been stopped.

MACDUFF
Your royal father has been murdered.

MALCOLM
Oh, by whom?

LENNOX
It appears that the servants in his room did it:
Their hands and faces were covered in blood;
so were their daggers, which they had left unwiped, upon their pillows: They stared at us with confusion when we went in. We shouldn't have trusted them with any man's life, let alone the king's.

MACBETH
But still, I regret the fury that made me kill them.

MACDUFF
Why did you do that?

MACBETH
Who can be wise, shocked, calm and furious, loyal and neutral all at the same moment? No one can: The love I have for Duncan caused me to act before I had time to think about what I was doing. Here lay Duncan, his silver skin covered in his own blood;
And his stab wounds looking like something unnatural and against nature and here were the two murderers, covered in the colour of their work – blood red, their daggers Covered in gore and blood: how could anyone who had a heart that loved Duncan and also the courage to show that love, not have done what I did?

LADY MACBETH
Help me away from here!

MACDUFF
Look after the lady.

MALCOLM

[Aside to DONALBAIN] Why do we hold our tongues,
That most may claim this argument for ours?

DONALBAIN

[Aside to MALCOLM] What should be spoken here,
where our fate,
Hid in an auger-hole, may rush, and seize us?
Let 's away;
Our tears are not yet brew'd.

MALCOLM

[Aside to DONALBAIN] Nor our strong sorrow
Upon the foot of motion.

BANQUO

Look to the lady:

LADY MACBETH is carried out

And when we have our naked frailties hid,
That suffer in exposure, let us meet,
And question this most bloody piece of work,
To know it further. Fears and scruples shake us:
In the great hand of God I stand; and thence
Against the undivulged pretence I fight
Of treasonous malice.

MACDUFF

And so do I.

ALL

So all.

MACBETH

Let's briefly put on manly readiness,
And meet i' the hall together.

ALL

Well contented.

Exeunt all but Malcolm and Donalbain.

MALCOLM

What will you do? Let's not consort with them:
To show an unfelt sorrow is an office
Which the false man does easy. I'll to England.

MALCOLM

[*Aside to DONALBAIN*] Why are we being so quiet,
We're the ones who should the most to say here?

DONALBAIN

[*Aside to Malcolm*] What can we say, especially here where we don't know what dangers are waiting to jump out at us?
Let's get away from here, we haven't even started grieving yet.

MALCOLM

[*Aside to DONALBAIN*] Our powerful sorrow is stronger than it appears, we have not yet even begun to take action.

BANQUO

Take care of the lady.

LADY MACBETH is carried out

And when we have dressed properly [they've all just gotten out of bed] for this cold, we can meet up and question what has happened here and try to figure it out. We are frightened by what has happened. By God, I will stand up against what has happened here and will try to uncover this treasonous act.

MACDUFF

And so do I.

ALL

So all.

MACBETH

Let's get dressed and meet up in the hall.

ALL

Agreed.

Exeunt all but MALCOLM and DONALBAIN

MALCOLM

What are you going to do? Let's not meet with them. It's very easy for a liar to pretend that he feels sorry. I'm going to go to England.

DONALBAIN

To Ireland, I; our separated fortune
Shall keep us both the safer: where we are,
There's daggers in men's smiles: the near in blood,
The nearer bloody.

MALCOLM

This murderous shaft that's shot
Hath not yet lighted, and our safest way
Is to avoid the aim. Therefore, to horse;
And let us not be dainty of leave-taking,
But shift away: there's warrant in that theft
Which steals itself, when there's no mercy left.

Exeunt

DONALBAIN

I'll go to Ireland; we're safer apart and away from here. Wherever we go people will be smiling at us but they will want to hurt us: our relatives are the people most likely to murder us.

MALCOLM

We haven't faced that challenge yet and it's best to steer clear of it. So let's get to our horses and there's no need for us to be polite about leaving – just go. We need to escape from here because there's no mercy to be felt anywhere.

Exeunt

ORIGINAL TEXT	MODERN TRANSLATION
Outside Macbeth's castle.	**Outside Macbeth's castle.**
Enter ROSS and an old Man	*Enter ROSS and an Old Man*
Old Man Threescore and ten I can remember well: Within the volume of which time I have seen Hours dreadful and things strange; but this sore night Hath trifled former knowings.	**Old Man** For seventy years I can remember everything that has happened. In that time, I have seen plenty of strange things and passed many dreadful hours but last night made everything else seem like a joke,
ROSS Ah, good father, Thou seest, the heavens, as troubled with man's act, Threaten his bloody stage: by the clock, 'tis day, And yet dark night strangles the travelling lamp: Is't night's predominance, or the day's shame, That darkness does the face of earth entomb, When living light should kiss it?	**ROSS** Yes, old man. You see the skies are troubled by the things men have done. By the clock, it should be day time but dark night is trying to put out the sun. Is it because night is so strong or daytime is so weak that darkness beings to spread out across the earth when it should still be daytime?
Old Man 'Tis unnatural, Even like the deed that's done. On Tuesday last, A falcon, towering in her pride of place, Was by a mousing owl hawk'd at and kill'd.	**Old Man** It's unnatural, just like the murder of the king. Last Tuesday, a falcon, flying high over the ground was caught and killed by an owl that usually goes after mice.
ROSS And Duncan's horses--a thing most strange and certain-- Beauteous and swift, the minions of their race, Turn'd wild in nature, broke their stalls, flung out, Contending 'gainst obedience, as they would make War with mankind.	**ROSS** And Duncan's horses – something very strange happened with them – beautiful and fast creatures, the finest of their kind, went wild and broke their stalls and wouldn't obey anyone as if they were trying to fight against all mankind.
Old Man 'Tis said they eat each other.	**Old Man** It's said that they tried to eat each other.
ROSS They did so, to the amazement of mine eyes That look'd upon't. Here comes the good Macduff.	**ROSS** They did, to my complete amazement as I watched on. Here comes the good Macduff

Enter MACDUFF	*Enter MACDUFF*
How goes the world, sir, now?	How is everything going now, sir?
MACDUFF Why, see you not?	**MACDUFF** Can you not see for yourself?
ROSS Is't known who did this more than bloody deed?	**ROSS** Is it known yet who committed the murder?
MACDUFF Those that Macbeth hath slain.	**MACDUFF** The men that Macbeth has killed.
ROSS Alas, the day! What good could they pretend?	**ROSS** Oh, what a shame! What could they have gained from killing Duncan?
MACDUFF They were suborn'd: Malcolm and Donalbain, the king's two sons, Are stol'n away and fled; which puts upon them Suspicion of the deed.	**MACDUFF** They were paid to do it: Malcolm and Donalbain, the king's two sons have slipped away and fled, which puts the suspicion on them.
ROSS 'Gainst nature still! Thriftless ambition, that wilt ravin up Thine own life's means! Then 'tis most like The sovereignty will fall upon Macbeth.	**ROSS** This is against the natural way of things. What kind of ambition will make someone kill the person who has given them life and supported them? It looks like Macbeth will become king.
MACDUFF He is already named, and gone to Scone To be invested.	**MACDUFF** He has already been named the new king and gone to Scone to be crowned.
ROSS Where is Duncan's body?	**ROSS** Where is Duncan's body?
MACDUFF Carried to Colmekill, The sacred storehouse of his predecessors, And guardian of their bones.	**MACDUFF** It's been taken to Colmekill, the place where his ancestors' bodies are kept.
ROSS Will you to Scone?	**ROSS** Will you go to Scone [for the crowning]?
MACDUFF No, cousin, I'll to Fife.	**MACDUFF** No, cousin, I'm going to go to Fife.
ROSS Well, I will thither.	**ROSS** Well, I'm going to go to Scone.

MACDUFF Well, may you see things well done there: adieu! Lest our old robes sit easier than our new! **ROSS** Farewell, father. **Old Man** God's benison go with you; and with those That would make good of bad, and friends of foes! *Exeunt*	**MACDUFF** I hope things go well there: see you soon. Hopefully things won't get any worse than they already are. **ROSS** Goodbye, old man. **Old Man** God's blessing go with you and with everyone who tries to turn bad things into good things and enemies into friends. *Exeunt*

Act 3 Scene 1

ORIGINAL TEXT	MODERN TRANSLATION
Forres. The palace.	**Forres. The palace.**
Enter BANQUO	*Enter BANQUO*
BANQUO Thou hast it now: king, Cawdor, Glamis, all, As the weird women promised, and, I fear, Thou play'dst most foully for't: yet it was said It should not stand in thy posterity, But that myself should be the root and father Of many kings. If there come truth from them-- As upon thee, Macbeth, their speeches shine-- Why, by the verities on thee made good, May they not be my oracles as well, And set me up in hope? But hush! no more.	**BANQUO** You have it all now, you're the king, the Lord of Cawdor and the Lord of Glamis, just as the witches promised, and I'm afraid that you did something really terrible to get it all. But it was also said that the crown wouldn't stay in your bloodline but that my children would be kings after you. If the first bit has been true then – which it clearly has for Macbeth – then the bit they said about my children must also be true, at least I hope it is. But quiet! No more of this.
Sennet sounded. Enter MACBETH, as king, LADY MACBETH, as queen, LENNOX, ROSS, Lords, Ladies, and Attendants	*Trumpet sounds. Enter MACBETH as the king, LADY MACBETH as queen, LENNOX, ROSS, Lords and ladies and Attendants*
MACBETH Here's our chief guest.	**MACBETH** Here's out main guest.
LADY MACBETH If he had been forgotten, It had been as a gap in our great feast, And all-thing unbecoming.	**LADY MACBETH** If we had forgotten about him, there would have been a huge gap in our celebratory feast and wholly inappropriate.
MACBETH To-night we hold a solemn supper sir, And I'll request your presence.	**MACBETH** Tonight we hold a formal dinner, sir, and I'm asking that you attend.
BANQUO Let your highness Command upon me; to the which my duties Are with a most indissoluble tie For ever knit.	**BANQUO** Command me to do whatever you wish and my duty is always to obey.
MACBETH Ride you this afternoon?	**MACBETH** Are you going out horse-riding today?
BANQUO Ay, my good lord.	**BANQUO** Yes my good lord.
MACBETH We should have else desired your good advice,	**MACBETH** We would have liked to hear your good advice, which has always been serious and beneficial,

Which still hath been both grave and prosperous,
In this day's council; but we'll take to-morrow.

Is't far you ride?

BANQUO
As far, my lord, as will fill up the time
'Twixt this and supper: go not my horse the better,
I must become a borrower of the night
For a dark hour or twain.

MACBETH
Fail not our feast.

BANQUO
My lord, I will not.

MACBETH
We hear, our bloody cousins are bestow'd
In England and in Ireland, not confessing
Their cruel parricide, filling their hearers
With strange invention: but of that to-morrow,
When therewithal we shall have cause of state
Craving us jointly. Hie you to horse: adieu,
Till you return at night. Goes Fleance with you?

BANQUO
Ay, my good lord: our time does call upon 's.

MACBETH
I wish your horses swift and sure of foot;
And so I do commend you to their backs.
Farewell.

Exit BANQUO

Let every man be master of his time
Till seven at night: to make society
The sweeter welcome, we will keep ourself
Till supper-time alone: while then, God be with you!

Exeunt all but MACBETH, and an attendant

Sirrah, a word with you: attend those men
Our pleasure?

---

in today's meeting; but we can hear what you have to say tomorrow.
Are you riding far?

BANQUO
As far, my Lord, as I can go between now and suppertime. If my horse is as fast as I know, I'll be back an hour or two after the sun has set.

MACBETH
Don't miss our banquet.

BANQUO
My lord, I will not.

MACBETH
I've heard that the two murdering princes are in England and Ireland. They haven't admitted to killing their father but they are telling the people they're saying with all sorts of crazy stories, but we can talk about that tomorrow at the meeting where we have to talk about matters of state. Hurry to your horse and I'll see you when you get back tonight.
Is Fleance going with you?

BANQUO
Yes, good lord: we have to go now.

MACBETH
I wish that your horses are fast and sure-footed and now, get on them. Goodbye.

Exit BANQUO

Everyone can do what they want with their time until seven o'clock: To make it more enjoyable to be in your company then, I'm going to be on my own until supper time. God be with you!

Exeunt all but MACBETH, and an attendant

You there, I want to speak with you: are those men there waiting for me?

ATTENDANT
They are, my lord, without the palace gate.

MACBETH
Bring them before us.

Exit Attendant

To be thus is nothing;
But to be safely thus.--Our fears in Banquo
Stick deep; and in his royalty of nature
Reigns that which would be fear'd: 'tis much he dares;
And, to that dauntless temper of his mind,
He hath a wisdom that doth guide his valour
To act in safety. There is none but he
Whose being I do fear: and, under him,
My Genius is rebuked; as, it is said,
Mark Antony's was by Caesar. He chid the sisters
When first they put the name of king upon me,
And bade them speak to him: then prophet-like
They hail'd him father to a line of kings:
Upon my head they placed a fruitless crown,
And put a barren sceptre in my gripe,
Thence to be wrench'd with an unlineal hand,
No son of mine succeeding. If 't be so,
For Banquo's issue have I filed my mind;
For them the gracious Duncan have I murder'd;
Put rancours in the vessel of my peace
Only for them; and mine eternal jewel
Given to the common enemy of man,
To make them kings, the seed of Banquo kings!
Rather than so, come fate into the list.
And champion me to the utterance! Who's there!

Re-enter Attendant, with two Murderers

Now go to the door, and stay there till we call.

Exit Attendant

Was it not yesterday we spoke together?

First Murderer
It was, so please your highness.

ATTENDANT
They are, my lord, just outside the palace gate.

MACBETH
Bring them to me.

Exit Attendant

To be the king is nothing unless I'm safe as well – my fear of Banquo runs deep; and in his personality there is something good and noble that I'm afraid of. He is willing to risk a lot added to that, his steady mind and his wisdom that guides his bravery to act always in the best way. There is no one else I fear as much as him and around him, my guiding spirit feels inferior in the same way as Mark Antony's did around Caesar.
He spoke out against the witches when they said that I would become king and told them to speak to him: then they told him a future where he would be father to a line of kings.
On my head they put a crown and in my hand they put a sceptre that I can't pass on to anyone. Someone unrelated to me will get these things after me because no son of mine will ever be king.
If that is true, it is for Banquo's sons that I have destroyed my conscience and murdered the gracious Duncan. I've unsettled my own peace of mind for their gain.
I have given my eternal soul to the devil to make Banquo's sons kings!
Rather than let that happen, I'm going to fight against fate and see who wins.
Who's there?

Re-enter Attendant, with two Murderers

Now go and wait by the door until we call you.

Exit Attendant

Wasn't it yesterday when we spoke to each other?

First Murderer
Yes, it was, your highness

MACBETH

Well then, now
Have you consider'd of my speeches? Know
That it was he in the times past which held you
So under fortune, which you thought had been
Our innocent self: this I made good to you
In our last conference, pass'd in probation with
you,
How you were borne in hand, how cross'd,
the instruments,
Who wrought with them, and all things else
that might
To half a soul and to a notion crazed
Say 'Thus did Banquo.'

First Murderer

You made it known to us.

MACBETH

I did so, and went further, which is now
Our point of second meeting. Do you find
Your patience so predominant in your nature
That you can let this go? Are you so gospell'd
To pray for this good man and for his issue,
Whose heavy hand hath bow'd you to the grave
And beggar'd yours for ever?

First Murderer

We are men, my liege.

MACBETH

Ay, in the catalogue ye go for men;
As hounds and greyhounds, mongrels, spaniels,
curs,
Shoughs, water-rugs and demi-wolves, are
clept
All by the name of dogs: the valued file
Distinguishes the swift, the slow, the subtle,
The housekeeper, the hunter, every one
According to the gift which bounteous nature
Hath in him closed; whereby he does receive
Particular addition. from the bill
That writes them all alike: and so of men.
Now, if you have a station in the file,
Not i' the worst rank of manhood, say 't;
And I will put that business in your bosoms,
Whose execution takes your enemy off,
Grapples you to the heart and love of us,
Who wear our health but sickly in his life,
Which in his death were perfect.

MACBETH

Well then, now have you considered what we
spoke about? Understand that it was Banquo
who prevented you, in the past, from living the
life that you deserved and not me, as you had
thought. I proved this to you the last time we
spoke, I showed you how you were deceived
and thwarted and what methods were used
against you and who was behind it. All of these
things would convince a half-wit or a madman
to say 'Banquo did it!'

First Murderer

You told us.

MACBETH

I did tell you, and then some, which is why we
are meeting for a second time.
Are you such patient men that you can ignore
this and let it go? Are you so righteous and holy
that you will pray for this man who has kept
you down and made you and your families
poor?

First Murderer

We are men, my lord.

MACBETH

Yes, in the general list of living things you are
called men, just like hounds, greyhounds,
mongrels, spaniels, water-dogs and wolfhounds
are all called dogs. But the really valuable list is
the one that classifies them according to their
natural gifts; which ones are fast, slow, clever,
protective, good at hunting and in this file each
dog is given a particular order.

And it is the same with men. Now, if you think
that you have a place in the rank order of men
that's not at the bottom, then tell me and I will
tell you something that will help you to get rid
of your enemy and bring you closer to my love.
While Banquo lives, it makes me feel sick; I will
not feel better until he is dead.

Second Murderer
I am one, my liege,
Whom the vile blows and buffets of the world
Have so incensed that I am reckless what
I do to spite the world.

First Murderer
And I another
So weary with disasters, tugg'd with fortune,
That I would set my lie on any chance,
To mend it, or be rid on't.

MACBETH
Both of you
Know Banquo was your enemy.

Both Murderers
True, my lord.

MACBETH
So is he mine; and in such bloody distance,
That every minute of his being thrusts
Against my near'st of life: and though I could
With barefaced power sweep him from my
sight
And bid my will avouch it, yet I must not,
For certain friends that are both his and mine,
Whose loves I may not drop, but wail his fall
Who I myself struck down; and thence it is,
That I to your assistance do make love,
Masking the business from the common eye
For sundry weighty reasons.

Second Murderer
We shall, my lord,
Perform what you command us.

First Murderer
Though our lives--

MACBETH
Your spirits shine through you. Within this hour
at most
I will advise you where to plant yourselves;
Acquaint you with the perfect spy o' the time,
The moment on't; for't must be done to-night,
And something from the palace; always
thought
That I require a clearness: and with him--
To leave no rubs nor botches in the work--

Second Murderer
I'm someone, my lord, who has been treated so
badly by this world that I don't care what I do
to spite it.

First Murderer
And I too, am someone so used to disaster and
misfortune that I would put my life on the line
for anything that might make my life a little bit
better.

MACBETH
Both of you know that Banquo was your
enemy.

Both Murderers
We do, my lord.

MACBETH
He is mine too and, like two fencers, every
minute that he lives thrusts towards me with a
sword. Although I could use my power as king
to get rid of him and no one could argue with
me, I can't because we have certain friends in
common that I need to keep on side. I have to
be able to wail and cry when I hear he's dead
even though I will have been the one who
ordered him killed. It is for that reason that I
now need your assistance.
I have to hide my real intentions and business
from everyone else for lots of important
reasons.

Second Murderer
We'll do what you ask of us, my Lord.

First Murderer
Although our lives…

MACBETH
I can see by looking at you what sort of men
you are. Within this hour, I will tell you where
to wait for him and when to do it because it has
to be done tonight.

It must also be done away from the palace
because I need to seem completely innocent.
Remember to kill both Banquo and Fleance,

Fleance his son, that keeps him company,
Whose absence is no less material to me
Than is his father's, must embrace the fate
Of that dark hour. Resolve yourselves apart:
I'll come to you anon.

Both Murderers
We are resolved, my lord.

MACBETH
I'll call upon you straight: abide within.

Exeunt Murderers

It is concluded. Banquo, thy soul's flight,
If it find heaven, must find it out to-night.

Exit

that is the plan and getting rid of Fleance is just
as important to me as killing Banquo.
Make up your minds separately whether you
want to do this and I'll come and find you
shortly.

Both Murderers
We have decided, my lord.

MACBETH
I'll call for you soon. Stay here.

Exeunt Murderers

It is finished. Banquo, if your soul is going to
heaven, it will have to find it tonight.

Exit

Act 3 Scene 2

ORIGINAL TEXT	MODERN TRANSLATION
The palace.	**The palace.**
Enter LADY MACBETH and a Servant	*Enter LADY MACBETH and a Servant*
LADY MACBETH Is Banquo gone from court?	**LADY MACBETH** Has Banquo left the castle?
Servant Ay, madam, but returns again to-night.	**Servant** Yes, madam, but he's coming back tonight.
LADY MACBETH Say to the king, I would attend his leisure For a few words.	**LADY MACBETH** Tell the king that I would like to speak to him briefly if he has the time.
Servant Madam, I will.	**Servant** I will, madam.
Exit	*Exit*
LADY MACBETH Nought's had, all's spent, Where our desire is got without content: 'Tis safer to be that which we destroy Than by destruction dwell in doubtful joy.	**LADY MACBETH** If we're not happy with what we've achieved and given everything to get it then it would be better to be the person who was murdered rather than the murderer who is tormented with anxiety.
Enter MACBETH	*Enter MACBETH*
How now, my lord! why do you keep alone, Of sorriest fancies your companions making, Using those thoughts which should indeed have died With them they think on? Things without all remedy Should be without regard: what's done is done.	How are you my Lord? Why are you keeping yourself all alone with only your dark and sorrowful thoughts to keep you company? Those thoughts and worries should have died with the men that they are about. There's no point in worrying about things you can't change. What's done is done.
MACBETH We have scotch'd the snake, not kill'd it: She'll close and be herself, whilst our poor malice Remains in danger of her former tooth. But let the frame of things disjoint, both the worlds suffer, Ere we will eat our meal in fear and sleep In the affliction of these terrible dreams That shake us nightly: better be with the dead,	**MACBETH** We have wounded the snake, not killed it: She will heal herself and go back to normal while we'll still be at risk of her biting us. But let the entire universe fall apart before I will eat my meals in fear and let these terrible nightmares keep me from sleep. I'd rather be dead along with the men we've killed than have to put up with this terrible mental torture and

Whom we, to gain our peace, have sent to peace,
Than on the torture of the mind to lie
In restless ecstasy. Duncan is in his grave;
After life's fitful fever he sleeps well;
Treason has done his worst: nor steel, nor poison,
Malice domestic, foreign levy, nothing,
Can touch him further.

LADY MACBETH
Come on;
Gentle my lord, sleek o'er your rugged looks;
Be bright and jovial among your guests to-night.

MACBETH
So shall I, love; and so, I pray, be you:
Let your remembrance apply to Banquo;
Present him eminence, both with eye and tongue:
Unsafe the while, that we
Must lave our honours in these flattering streams,
And make our faces vizards to our hearts,
Disguising what they are.

LADY MACBETH
You must leave this.

MACBETH
O, full of scorpions is my mind, dear wife!
Thou know'st that Banquo, and his Fleance, lives.

LADY MACBETH
But in them nature's copy's not eterne.

MACBETH
There's comfort yet; they are assailable;
Then be thou jocund: ere the bat hath flown
His cloister'd flight, ere to black Hecate's summons
The shard-borne beetle with his drowsy hums
Hath rung night's yawning peal, there shall be done
A deed of dreadful note.

LADY MACBETH
What's to be done?

being unable to sleep, which we did for our own peace.

Duncan is in his grave:
The troubles of his life are over and he sleeps well. We've done the worst we possibly could to him, nothing else can hurt him now, not poison, nor the blade of a knife or a sword, nor rebellions nor invasion.

LADY MACBETH
Come on, calm down my lord. Gloss over your unhappy looks. Be happy and cheerful for your guests that are coming tonight.

MACBETH
I will, my love and you should do the same: Make sure that you treat Banquo well, say nice things about him and make sure he wants for nothing:

We're not safe at the moment and we must put off suspicion by speaking hiding our true feelings and intentions.

LADY MACBETH
You have to stop talking about this.

MACBETH
Oh, my mind is full of scorpions my dear wife! You know that Banquo and his son, Fleance, are alive.

LADY MACBETH
But they can't live forever.

MACBETH
There's comfort in that thought; they are able to be killed;
Be happy wife: before the bat has flown from here to answer the goddess Hecate's call, before the beetle has made its humming noise like a bell saying it's nightime, a dreadful deed will be done.

LADY MACBETH
What are you going to do?

MACBETH	**MACBETH**
Be innocent of the knowledge, dearest chuck,	It's better you don't know dear until after it's
Till thou applaud the deed. Come, seeling night,	done and you are happy about it. Come dark of
Scarf up the tender eye of pitiful day;	night and cover up the tender eye of pitiful day
And with thy bloody and invisible hand	and with your bloody and invisible hand, rip up
Cancel and tear to pieces that great bond	Banquo's life contract which, while it exists and
Which keeps me pale! Light thickens; and the crow	he's alive, worries me!
Makes wing to the rooky wood:	The sky is darkening and the crow flies into the
Good things of day begin to droop and drowse;	woods. The good things of the day time begin
While night's black agents to their preys do rouse.	to get sleepy while the agents of darkness awake to hunt.
Thou marvell'st at my words: but hold thee still;	You are amazed by my words but be still for a bit.
Things bad begun make strong themselves by ill.	Once you commit bad deeds, you are forced to
So, prithee, go with me.	carry out more bad deeds. So, please, come with me.
Exeunt	*Exeunt*

Act 3 Scene 3

ORIGINAL TEXT	MODERN TRANSLATION
A park near the palace.	**A park near the palace.**
Enter three Murderers	*Enter three murderers*
First Murderer But who did bid thee join with us?	**First Murderer** But who told you to join us?
Third Murderer Macbeth.	**Third Murderer** Macbeth.
Second Murderer He needs not our mistrust, since he delivers Our offices and what we have to do To the direction just.	**Second Murderer** We can probably trust this man seeing as he has been given the same orders as we have.
First Murderer Then stand with us. The west yet glimmers with some streaks of day: Now spurs the lated traveller apace To gain the timely inn; and near approaches The subject of our watch.	**First Murderer** Stay with us then. There is still some light in the sky: Now the last of the evening's travellers are hurrying towards their inns; and nearby comes the person we are looking for.
Third Murderer Hark! I hear horses.	**Third Murderer** Listen! I hear horses.
BANQUO [*Within*] Give us a light there, ho!	**BANQUO** [*Within*] Give us a light here!
Second Murderer Then 'tis he: the rest That are within the note of expectation Already are i' the court.	**Second Murderer** Then it's him. The rest of the guests that are expected are already inside.
First Murderer His horses go about.	**First Murderer** I can hear his and Fleance's horses.
Third Murderer Almost a mile: but he does usually, So all men do, from hence to the palace gate Make it their walk.	**Third Murderer** It's almost a mile from here to the palace gate but nearly everyone walks it, as Banquo is going to do now.
Second Murderer A light, a light!	**Second Murderer** Get some light here, light!

Enter BANQUO, and FLEANCE with a torch	*Enter BANQUO and FLEANCE with a torch*
Third Murderer 'Tis he.	**Third Murderer** It's him.
First Murderer Stand to't.	**First Murderer** Get ready.
BANQUO It will be rain to-night.	**BANQUO** It's going to rain tonight.
First Murderer Let it come down.	**First Murderer** Then let it come down.
They set upon BANQUO	*They set upon BANQUO*
BANQUO O, treachery! Fly, good Fleance, fly, fly, fly! Thou mayst revenge. O slave!	**BANQUO** Oh, this is treachery! Run, good Fleance, run, run, run! You may revenge my death one day. Oh, you slave!
Dies. FLEANCE escapes	*Dies. FLEANCE escapes*
Third Murderer Who did strike out the light?	**Third Murderer** Who put out the light?
First Murderer Wast not the way?	**First Murderer** Was that not what we had planned?
Third Murderer There's but one down; the son is fled.	**Third Murderer** There's only one dead, the son got away.
Second Murderer We have lost Best half of our affair.	**Second Murderer** We've only completed part of the mission.
First Murderer Well, let's away, and say how much is done.	**First Murderer** Let's go to tell Macbeth about what we've done.
Exeunt	*Exeunt*

Act 3 Scene 4

ORIGINAL TEXT	MODERN TRANSLATION
The same. Hall in the palace.	**The same. Hall in the palace.**
A banquet prepared. Enter MACBETH, LADY MACBETH, ROSS, LENNOX, Lords, and Attendants	*A banquet prepared. Enter MACBETH, LADY MACBETH, ROSS, LENNOX, Lords and Attendants.*
MACBETH You know your own degrees; sit down: at first And last the hearty welcome.	**MACBETH** You all know your own rank, sit down accordingly and from the highest to the lowest, I welcome all of you heartily.
Lords Thanks to your majesty.	**Lords** Thanks, your majesty.
MACBETH Ourself will mingle with society, And play the humble host. Our hostess keeps her state, but in best time We will require her welcome.	**MACBETH** I will mingle with you all and be a good host. My wife will stay on the throne for now but, when I ask her to, she will also come and welcome you.
LADY MACBETH Pronounce it for me, sir, to all our friends; For my heart speaks they are welcome.	**LADY MACBETH** Welcome them all for me, sir, because my heart says they are welcome.
First Murderer appears at the door	*First murderer appears at the door*
MACBETH See, they encounter thee with their hearts' thanks. Both sides are even: here I'll sit i' the midst: Be large in mirth; anon we'll drink a measure The table round. *Approaching the door* There's blood on thy face.	**MACBETH** And they respond to you with their hearts also, both sides of the table are full now: I will sit in the middle. Enjoy yourselves! Shortly we will drink a toast around the table. *Approaching the door* There's blood on your face.
First Murderer 'Tis Banquo's then.	**First Murderer** It's Banquo's blood.
MACBETH 'Tis better thee without than he within. Is he dispatch'd?	**MACBETH** It's better that it's on your face than running through him keeping him alive. Is he dead?
First Murderer My lord, his throat is cut; that I did for him.	**First Murderer** My lord, his throat has been cut; I did it myself.

MACBETH
Thou art the best o' the cut-throats: yet he's good
That did the like for Fleance: if thou didst it,
Thou art the nonpareil.

First Murderer
Most royal sir,
Fleance is 'scaped.

MACBETH
Then comes my fit again: I had else been perfect,
Whole as the marble, founded as the rock,
As broad and general as the casing air:
But now I am cabin'd, cribb'd, confined, bound in
To saucy doubts and fears. But Banquo's safe?

First Murderer
Ay, my good lord: safe in a ditch he bides,
With twenty trenched gashes on his head;
The least a death to nature.

MACBETH
Thanks for that:
There the grown serpent lies; the worm that's fled
Hath nature that in time will venom breed,
No teeth for the present. Get thee gone: to-morrow
We'll hear, ourselves, again.

Exit Murderer

LADY MACBETH
My royal lord,
You do not give the cheer: the feast is sold
That is not often vouch'd, while 'tis a-making,
'Tis given with welcome: to feed were best at home;
From thence the sauce to meat is ceremony;
Meeting were bare without it.

MACBETH
Sweet remembrancer!
Now, good digestion wait on appetite,
And health on both!

MACBETH
You are the best of the throat-cutters but whoever has done the same for Fleance is also a good throat cutter. If you did both, then you are peerless.

First Murderer
Most royal sir,
Fleance has escaped.

MACBETH
Then I'm worried again: if he were dead I would be perfect, as strong as marble, as steady as a foundation in rock, as free and happy as the breeze but now I'm caught up in all my anxieties again. But Banquo's definitely dead?

First Murderer
Yes, my good lord: dead in a ditch he is with twenty wounds to his head; the smallest of which would have been enough to kill him.

MACBETH
Thanks for that: so the adult snake lies dead in a ditch; the baby snake has fled away. In time he will grow poisonous but for now he does not have fangs. Go away from here, we'll talk again tomorrow.

Exit Murderer

LADY MACBETH
My royal lord, you're not paying your guests enough attention: they're going to begin to feel like they're paying for their meal if you don't make them feel welcome. If you just want to eat food, it's better to do that in your own home, but when you eat with other people it's important to make it an occasion otherwise dinner parties wouldn't be enjoyable.

MACBETH
Thank you for reminding me! Now, good digestion requires a good appetite and good health depends on both!

LENNOX May't please your highness sit.	**LENNOX** Please your highness, sit.
The GHOST OF BANQUO enters, and sits in MACBETH's place	*The GHOST OF BANQUO enters and sits in MACBETH'S place*
MACBETH Here had we now our country's honour roof'd, Were the graced person of our Banquo present; Who may I rather challenge for unkindness Than pity for mischance!	**MACBETH** We would have all the nobility of our country here under one roof if Banquo too were present; I hope that it turns out that he is late because he is being rude rather than anything bad has happened to him.
ROSS His absence, sir, Lays blame upon his promise. Please't your highness To grace us with your royal company.	**ROSS** His absence, sir, means that he has broken his promise. Please sit with us your highness and grace us with your royal company.
MACBETH The table's full.	**MACBETH** The table's full.
LENNOX Here is a place reserved, sir.	**LENNOX** Here is a place we've kept for you sir.
MACBETH Where?	**MACBETH** Where?
LENNOX Here, my good lord. What is't that moves your highness?	**LENNOX** Here, my good lord. What is it that upsets you, your highness?
MACBETH Which of you have done this?	**MACBETH** Which one of you has done this?
Lords What, my good lord?	**Lords** What, my good lord?
MACBETH Thou canst not say I did it: never shake Thy gory locks at me.	**MACBETH** [*to the GHOST*] You can't blame it on me: Don't shake your bloody head at me.
ROSS Gentlemen, rise: his highness is not well.	**ROSS** Gentlemen, let's go: his highness is not well.
LADY MACBETH Sit, worthy friends: my lord is often thus, And hath been from his youth: pray you, keep seat; The fit is momentary; upon a thought He will again be well: if much you note him,	**LADY MACBETH** Sit down good friends: my lord is often like this and has been since he was a young child. Please, stay where you are. What he is experiencing will pass quickly, after a moment, he will be himself again.

You shall offend him and extend his passion:
Feed, and regard him not. Are you a man?

MACBETH
Ay, and a bold one, that dare look on that
Which might appal the devil.

LADY MACBETH
O proper stuff!
This is the very painting of your fear:
This is the air-drawn dagger which, you said,
Led you to Duncan. O, these flaws and starts,
Impostors to true fear, would well become
A woman's story at a winter's fire,
Authorized by her grandam. Shame itself!
Why do you make such faces? When all's done,
You look but on a stool.

MACBETH
Prithee, see there! behold! look! lo!
how say you?
Why, what care I? If thou canst nod, speak too.
If charnel-houses and our graves must send
Those that we bury back, our monuments
Shall be the maws of kites.

GHOST OF BANQUO vanishes

LADY MACBETH
What, quite unmann'd in folly?

MACBETH
If I stand here, I saw him.

LADY MACBETH
Fie, for shame!

MACBETH
Blood hath been shed ere now, i' the olden time,
Ere human statute purged the gentle weal;
Ay, and since too, murders have been perform'd
Too terrible for the ear: the times have been,
That, when the brains were out, the man would die,
And there an end; but now they rise again,
With twenty mortal murders on their crowns,

If you pay too much attention to him you'll only upset him even more.
Eat and don't look at him. [*To MACBETH*] Are you a man?

MACBETH
Yes, and a tough one too who can look on that thing that would frighten the devil.

LADY MACBETH
Oh will you stop this nonsense! This is just another hallucination you get when you're afraid - just like the dagger that you said led you to Duncan. These episodes don't even look like you're really afraid. It's like you're pretending, just like a woman might who was telling scary stories by the fire to her grandmother. Shame on you! When this is over, you'll see that all you're looking at is a stool.

MACBETH
Please, look over there! Look! See! There! What do you say now? Why, what do I care? If you can nod at me then speak.
If the dead can simply return from their graves then there's nothing to stop the birds from pecking at them. So there's no point in burying them at all.

GHOST OF BANQUO vanishes

LADY MACBETH
Has this madness completely paralyzed you?

MACBETH
As I'm standing here, I saw him.

LADY MACBETH
Stop this, it's embarrassing.

MACBETH
In the olden times, before there were laws to keep the land safe and peaceful, much blood was spilled. And since then too, some awful murders have been committed. But before, the murdered man would die and that would be the end of it but now they rise again and with twenty deadly wounds on their heads, they push us from our stools and come back to haunt us. This is worse than the murder itself.

And push us from our stools: this is more strange
Than such a murder is.

LADY MACBETH
My worthy lord,
Your noble friends do lack you.

MACBETH
I do forget.
Do not muse at me, my most worthy friends,
I have a strange infirmity, which is nothing
To those that know me. Come, love and health to all;
Then I'll sit down. Give me some wine; fill full.
I drink to the general joy o' the whole table,
And to our dear friend Banquo, whom we miss;
Would he were here! to all, and him, we thirst,
And all to all.

Lords
Our duties, and the pledge.

Re-enter GHOST OF BANQUO

MACBETH
Avaunt! and quit my sight! let the earth hide thee!
Thy bones are marrowless, thy blood is cold;
Thou hast no speculation in those eyes
Which thou dost glare with!

LADY MACBETH
Think of this, good peers,
But as a thing of custom: 'tis no other;
Only it spoils the pleasure of the time.

MACBETH
What man dare, I dare:
Approach thou like the rugged Russian bear,
The arm'd rhinoceros, or the Hyrcan tiger;
Take any shape but that, and my firm nerves
Shall never tremble: or be alive again,
And dare me to the desert with thy sword;
If trembling I inhabit then, protest me
The baby of a girl. Hence, horrible shadow!
Unreal mockery, hence!

GHOST OF BANQUO vanishes

LADY MACBETH
My good lord, you're neglecting your guests.

MACBETH
You're right, I've forgotten about them. Do not pay any attention to me my friends, I have a strange condition which those who know me well have become used to. Come, a toast to love and health to everyone: now I'll sit with you. Give me some wine, fill up my glass. I drink to the happiness of everyone seated here at the table and to our dear friend Banquo who's not here yet but we wish were here! To all of you here, and him, we drink!

Lords
Hear, hear.

Re-enter GHOST OF BANQUO

MACBETH
Go! Get out of here! Get back into your grave!

There is no life in your bones, your blood is cold, you can't see from your eyes with which you glare at me!

LADY MACBETH
Think of this, my good friends, as simply a bad habit: it's nothing except it spoils our nice evening.

MACBETH
I'm as brave as any other man. Come at me like a rugged Russian bear, a thick-skinned rhinoceros or the Iranian tiger. Come at me as anything but a ghost and I would not be afraid. Or come back to life and challenge me to a sword fight in some remote place and if I tremble you can say I'm a little girl.
Get out of here horrible ghost! Get out mocking hallucination!

GHOST OF BANQUO vanishes

Why, so: being gone,
I am a man again. Pray you, sit still.

LADY MACBETH
You have displaced the mirth, broke the good meeting,
With most admired disorder.

MACBETH
Can such things be,
And overcome us like a summer's cloud,
Without our special wonder? You make me strange
Even to the disposition that I owe,
When now I think you can behold such sights,
And keep the natural ruby of your cheeks,
When mine is blanched with fear.

ROSS
What sights, my lord?

LADY MACBETH
I pray you, speak not; he grows worse and worse;
Question enrages him. At once, good night:
Stand not upon the order of your going,
But go at once.

LENNOX
Good night; and better health
Attend his majesty!

LADY MACBETH
A kind good night to all!

Exeunt all but MACBETH and LADY MACBETH

MACBETH
It will have blood; they say, blood will have blood:
Stones have been known to move and trees to speak;
Augurs and understood relations have
By magot-pies and choughs and rooks brought forth
The secret'st man of blood. What is the night?

LADY MACBETH
Almost at odds with morning, which is which.

Why, now that it's gone I am a man again.
Please, friends, stay where you are.

LADY MACBETH
You have spoiled the evening's fun, wrecked the atmosphere with your little show.

MACBETH
Can these things come upon me so suddenly without shocking any of the rest of you? You make me feel like I don't know myself when all of you can look upon such sights and not be upset in the slightest while I'm pale with fright.

ROSS
What sights, my lord?

LADY MACBETH
Please, don't speak about it; he is getting worse;
Questions anger him. Good night to all of you now, don't leave according to your rank, just leave at once.

LENNOX
Good night and I hope his majesty feels better soon.

LADY MACBETH
A kind good night to all of you!

Exeunt all but MACBETH and LADY MACBETH

MACBETH
It is said that the dead will have their revenge, blood will cause more blood. Gravestones have been known to move and trees to speak to bring guilty men to justice. The best kept secrets of men have been exposed by magical signs made by crows and rooks.
How late in the night is it?

LADY MACBETH
It's nearly morning. It's difficult to tell if it's day or night.

MACBETH

How say'st thou, that Macduff denies his person
At our great bidding?

LADY MACBETH

Did you send to him, sir?

MACBETH

I hear it by the way; but I will send:
There's not a one of them but in his house
I keep a servant fee'd. I will to-morrow,
And betimes I will, to the weird sisters:
More shall they speak; for now I am bent to know,
By the worst means, the worst. For mine own good,
All causes shall give way: I am in blood
Stepp'd in so far that, should I wade no more,
Returning were as tedious as go o'er:
Strange things I have in head, that will to hand;
Which must be acted ere they may be scann'd.

LADY MACBETH

You lack the season of all natures, sleep.

MACBETH

Come, we'll to sleep. My strange and self-abuse
Is the initiate fear that wants hard use:
We are yet but young in deed.

Exeunt

MACBETH

What do you think of the fact that Macduff doesn't do as we ask him to?

LADY MACBETH

Did you send for him, sir?

MACBETH

I've heard about it from other people, but I will send for him: I keep a servant as a spy in all of the lords' houses. Tomorrow, I will go to see the witches again and get them to tell me more because I want to know the worst that will happen.
My own safety is the only thing I care about at the moment. Everything else comes second. I have waded into this river of blood to the point where it's just as easy to keep going and keep killing than it is to go back to the way things were before.
I have some ideas in my head and, because they are terrible, I need to just do them before I think too much about them.

LADY MACBETH

You haven't slept enough.

MACBETH

Come, let's go to sleep. My strange moods and hallucinations are because we're only beginners in crime. It will get easier with practice.

Exeunt

ORIGINAL TEXT	MODERN TRANSLATION
A Heath.	**A HEATH**
Thunder. Enter the three Witches meeting HECATE	*Thunder. Enter the three Witches meeting HECATE*
First Witch Why, how now, Hecate! you look angerly.	**First Witch** How are you, Hecate! You look angry!
HECATE Have I not reason, beldams as you are, Saucy and overbold? How did you dare To trade and traffic with Macbeth In riddles and affairs of death; And I, the mistress of your charms, The close contriver of all harms, Was never call'd to bear my part, Or show the glory of our art? And, which is worse, all you have done Hath been but for a wayward son, Spiteful and wrathful, who, as others do, Loves for his own ends, not for you. But make amends now: get you gone, And at the pit of Acheron Meet me i' the morning: thither he Will come to know his destiny: Your vessels and your spells provide, Your charms and every thing beside. I am for the air; this night I'll spend Unto a dismal and a fatal end: Great business must be wrought ere noon: Upon the corner of the moon There hangs a vaporous drop profound; I'll catch it ere it come to ground: And that distill'd by magic sleights Shall raise such artificial sprites As by the strength of their illusion Shall draw him on to his confusion: He shall spurn fate, scorn death, and bear He hopes 'bove wisdom, grace and fear: And you all know, security Is mortals' chiefest enemy.	**HECATE** Do I not have a reason to be angry, you disobedient old women? How dare you speak to Macbeth and give him riddles and prophecies to do with his future without first consulting me, the source of all your powers. I'm the one who decides what evil things happen in the world but you didn't summon me to take part and show how powerful I am. And what is worse, you've done all of this for a man who is hateful, jealous, and evil and does things for his own benefit, not for any of you. But you can save this situation. Go away and meet me tomorrow morning at the pit of Acheron. Macbeth will arrive there to find out what lies in store for him. Bring your cauldrons, your spells, your charms and everything else you have. I'm going now. Tonight I'll work out some terrible thing we can do. I've much to do before noon. From the corner of the moon hangs an important droplet. I'll catch it before it falls to earth and work on it with magic tricks and create visions that will confuse Macbeth. They will trick him into ignoring fate and believing that nothing can harm him. As we all know, that is life's biggest enemy.
Music and a song within: 'Come away, come away,' & c	*Music and a song within. 'Come away, come away'*

Hark! I am call'd; my little spirit, see, Sits in a foggy cloud, and stays for me. *Exit* **First Witch** Come, let's make haste; she'll soon be back again. *Exeunt*	Listen! I'm being called. See, my little spirit waits in the clouds for me. *Exit* **First Witch** Let's go quickly, she'll be back again soon. *Exeunt*

ORIGINAL TEXT	MODERN TRANSLATION
Forres. The palace.	**Forres. The palace.**
Enter LENNOX and another Lord	*Enter LENNOX and another Lord*
LENNOX	**LENNOX**
My former speeches have but hit your thoughts,	What I have spoken before shows me that we both are thinking along the same lines. Lately, very strange things have been happening. The gracious Duncan was very much pitied by Macbeth, although he was dead at the time. And the good and noble Banquo was out walking too late at night!
Which can interpret further: only, I say,	
Things have been strangely borne. The gracious Duncan	
Was pitied of Macbeth: marry, he was dead:	
And the right-valiant Banquo walk'd too late;	
Whom, you may say, if't please you, Fleance kill'd,	If you want, we can say that Fleance killed his father because he did run away afterwards. Men must not go out walking too late at night. And it must be said that it was a monstrous things for Malcolm and Donalbain to kill their own father! What a terrible thing! How it upset Macbeth. Didn't he, full of rage, go and kill the two servants who were still drunk and asleep at the time. That was loyal of him. And it was wise too because it would have caused the rest of us such anger to hear those men say they didn't do it.
For Fleance fled: men must not walk too late.	
Who cannot want the thought how monstrous	
It was for Malcolm and for Donalbain	
To kill their gracious father? damned fact!	
How it did grieve Macbeth! did he not straight	
In pious rage the two delinquents tear,	
That were the slaves of drink and thralls of sleep?	
Was not that nobly done? Ay, and wisely too;	
For 'twould have anger'd any heart alive	
To hear the men deny't. So that, I say,	
He has borne all things well: and I do think	So I say he has done everything correctly. If he had Duncan's sons locked up somewhere, and it's a good thing that he doesn't, they too would find out how awful the punishment is for those who kill their own fathers and Fleance would too.
That had he Duncan's sons under his key--	
As, an't please heaven, he shall not--they should find	
What 'twere to kill a father; so should Fleance.	
But, peace! for from broad words and 'cause he fail'd	But enough of this talk, I hear that Macduff has upset the king because he speaks his thoughts too openly and did not attend Macbeth's feast when he was invited.
His presence at the tyrant's feast, I hear	
Macduff lives in disgrace: sir, can you tell	
Where he bestows himself?	Can you tell me anymore about this? Where is he keeping himself?
Lord	**Lord**
The son of Duncan,	Malcolm, Duncan's son and the rightful heir to the throne and from whom Macbeth has stolen it, is living with the King of England and, despite his misfortunes, is highly respected down there. Macduff has gone there to ask the King of England to join forces with the Earl of Northumberland and his warrior son, Siward.
From whom this tyrant holds the due of birth	
Lives in the English court, and is received	
Of the most pious Edward with such grace	
That the malevolence of fortune nothing	
Takes from his high respect: thither Macduff	
Is gone to pray the holy king, upon his aid	

To wake Northumberland and warlike Siward:
That, by the help of these--with Him above
To ratify the work--we may again
Give to our tables meat, sleep to our nights,
Free from our feasts and banquets bloody
knives,
Do faithful homage and receive free honours:
All which we pine for now: and this report
Hath so exasperate the king that he
Prepares for some attempt of war.

LENNOX
Sent he to Macduff?

Lord
He did: and with an absolute 'Sir, not I,'
The cloudy messenger turns me his back,
And hums, as who should say 'You'll rue the
time
That clogs me with this answer.'

LENNOX
And that well might
Advise him to a caution, to hold what distance
His wisdom can provide. Some holy angel
Fly to the court of England and unfold
His message ere he come, that a swift blessing
May soon return to this our suffering country
Under a hand accursed!

Lord
I'll send my prayers with him.

Exeunt

Macduff hopes that with their help, and the
help of God, we may again be able to put food
on our tables, bring peace to our nights, free
our celebrations and days from bloody knives
and so that we can pay homage to our dead
king and receive honours freely. All of these
things, we long for at the moment. Macbeth
has heard of this plan and is so angry about it
that he has begun to prepare for war.

LENNOX
Did he send for Macduff to come back?

Lord
He did and he told the messenger 'no way'. The
angry messenger turned his back on Macduff
almost as if to say 'you'll regret that answer
you've given me.'

LENNOX
That will probably cause Macduff to stay in
England and keep his distance. Some holy angel
should fly to England to tell him to come back
to Scotland quickly to free his country because
it is suffering under the leadership of a cursed
tyrant!

Lord
I'll send my prayers with him.

Exeunt

ORIGINAL TEXT	MODERN TRANSLATION
A cavern. In the middle, a boiling cauldron.	**A cavern. In the middle there is a boiling cauldron.**
Thunder. Enter the three Witches	*Thunder. Enter the three witches*
First Witch Thrice the brinded cat hath mew'd.	**First Witch** The tabby cat has meowed three times.
Second Witch Thrice and once the hedge-pig whined.	**Second Witch** The hedgehog has whined four times.
Third Witch Harpier cries 'Tis time, 'tis time.	**Third Witch** The beast with woman's body and animal's wings cries: "It's time, it's time".
First Witch Round about the cauldron go; In the poison'd entrails throw. Toad, that under cold stone Days and nights has thirty-one Swelter'd venom sleeping got, Boil thou first i' the charmed pot.	**First witch** Around the cauldron we go: Throw in some poisoned internal organs. A toad, who sat under a cold rock for thirty-one days sweating out venom, goes in first.
ALL Double, double toil and trouble; Fire burn, and cauldron bubble.	**ALL** Double, double toil and trouble; Fire burn and cauldron bubble.
Second Witch Fillet of a fenny snake, In the cauldron boil and bake; Eye of newt and toe of frog, Wool of bat and tongue of dog, Adder's fork and blind-worm's sting, Lizard's leg and owlet's wing, For a charm of powerful trouble, Like a hell-broth boil and bubble.	**Second witch** Next goes a slice of snake from the marshes, into the cauldron to boil and bake; After that we put in the eye of a newt and the toe of a frog; some wool from a bat and the tongue of a dog; the forked tongue from an adder and a blind worm's sting; a lizard's leg and a baby owl's wing. All this goes in for a powerful spell that is as terrible as if it were made in hell itself.
ALL Double, double toil and trouble; Fire burn and cauldron bubble.	**ALL** Double, double toil and trouble; Fire burn and cauldron bubble.
Third Witch Scale of dragon, tooth of wolf, Witches' mummy, maw and gulf Of the ravin'd salt-sea shark,	**Third Witch** I'm going to put in: a scale from a dragon's skin, the tooth from a wolf, a witch's mummified skin, the stomach and gullet of a shark, root of

Root of hemlock digg'd i' the dark,
Liver of blaspheming Jew,
Gall of goat, and slips of yew
Silver'd in the moon's eclipse,
Nose of Turk and Tartar's lips,
Finger of birth-strangled babe
Ditch-deliver'd by a drab,
Make the gruel thick and slab:
Add thereto a tiger's chaudron,
For the ingredients of our cauldron.

ALL
Double, double toil and trouble;
Fire burn and cauldron bubble.

Second Witch
Cool it with a baboon's blood,
Then the charm is firm and good.

Enter HECATE to the other three Witches

HECATE
O well done! I commend your pains;
And every one shall share i' the gains;
And now about the cauldron sing,
Live elves and fairies in a ring,
Enchanting all that you put in.

Music and a song: 'Black spirits,' & c

HECATE retires

Second Witch
By the pricking of my thumbs,
Something wicked this way comes.
Open, locks,
Whoever knocks!

Enter MACBETH

MACBETH
How now, you secret, black, and midnight hags!
What is't you do?

ALL
A deed without a name.

---

hemlock which has been dug up at night. The
liver of a Jew who swears against God, bile
from a goat's stomach and cuttings from the
yew tree gotten during an eclipse, a Turk's
nose, a Tartar's lips; the finger of a baby who
died in childbirth to a prostitute; Make this
potion thick and sticky and to it we'll add a
tiger's entrails.

ALL
Double, double toil and trouble;
Fire burn and cauldron bubble.

Second witch
Cool the mixture with the blood from a baboon
and then the potion is almost ready.

Enter HECATE to the other three witches

HECATE
Oh well done! I congratulate you on the efforts
you have gone to and all of you will share the
rewards from it;
Now let's gather around the cauldron and sing
our spell, like magical beings in a ring
enchanting everything that goes in.

HECATE retires

Second Witch
By the tingling sensation in my thumbs, I think
that something wicked is coming this way.
Doors, open your locks for whoever it is that
knocks.

Enter MACBETH

MACBETH
How are you now, you secret, black and
midnight hags?
What are you doing?

ALL
Something there is no name for.

MACBETH
I conjure you, by that which you profess,
Howe'er you come to know it, answer me:
Though you untie the winds and let them fight
Against the churches; though the yesty waves
Confound and swallow navigation up;
Though bladed corn be lodged and trees blown
down;
Though castles topple on their warders' heads;
Though palaces and pyramids do slope
Their heads to their foundations; though the
treasure
Of nature's germens tumble all together,
Even till destruction sicken; answer me
To what I ask you.

First Witch
Speak.

Second Witch
Demand.

Third Witch
We'll answer.

First Witch
Say, if thou'dst rather hear it from our mouths,
Or from our masters?

MACBETH
Call 'em; let me see 'em.

First Witch
Pour in sow's blood, that hath eaten
Her nine farrow; grease that's sweaten
From the murderer's gibbet throw
Into the flame.

ALL
Come, high or low;
Thyself and office deftly show!

Thunder. First Apparition: an armed Head

MACBETH
Tell me, thou unknown power,--

First Witch
He knows thy thought:
Hear his speech, but say thou nought.

MACBETH
I call on you, by the powers that rule you, to
answer my questions, however it is you know
the answers.
Even if it means that you unleash ferocious
winds that knock down churches and whip up
foamy waves that drown sailors at sea; even if
it destroys crops and knocks down trees; even
if it flattens castles, bringing them down upon
the heads of the people inside; even if it brings
palaces and pyramids to the ground; even if it
turns everything in nature upside down, tell me
what I want to know.

First Witch
Speak

Second Witch
Demand

Third Witch
We'll answer

First Witch
Tell us if you would prefer us to tell you these
answers or if you want to hear it from our
masters.

MACBETH
Call them, let me see them.

First Witch
Pour in the blood of a pig that has eaten her
nine babies; add to it the sweat of a man
hanged on the gallows and throw it into the
flame.

ALL
Come, spirits, high or low and show what you
can do.

Thunder. First Apparition: and armed Head

MACBETH
Tell me, you mysterious power...

First Witch
He can read your mind, there's no need to
speak, just listen.

First Apparition
Macbeth! Macbeth! Macbeth! beware
Macduff;
Beware the thane of Fife. Dismiss me. Enough.

Descends

MACBETH
Whate'er thou art, for thy good caution,
thanks;
Thou hast harp'd my fear aright: but one
word more,--

First Witch
He will not be commanded: here's another,
More potent than the first.

Thunder. Second Apparition: A bloody Child

Second Apparition
Macbeth! Macbeth! Macbeth!

MACBETH
Had I three ears, I'ld hear thee.

Second Apparition
Be bloody, bold, and resolute; laugh to scorn
The power of man, for none of woman born
Shall harm Macbeth.

Descends

MACBETH
Then live, Macduff: what need I fear of thee?
But yet I'll make assurance double sure,
And take a bond of fate: thou shalt not live;
That I may tell pale-hearted fear it lies,
And sleep in spite of thunder.

*Thunder. Third Apparition: a Child crowned,
with a tree in his hand*

What is this
That rises like the issue of a king,
And wears upon his baby-brow the round
And top of sovereignty?

ALL
Listen, but speak not to't.

First Apparition
Macbeth! Macbeth! Macbeth! Beware
Macduff; Beware the thane of Fife. Dismiss me.
Enough.

Descends

MACBETH
Whatever you are, for your warning, I thank
you. You have guessed my fear correctly but
tell me something else...

First Witch
He will not be commanded to do anything:
here's another, stronger than the first.

Thunder. Second Apparition: A bloody child

Second Apparition
Macbeth! Macbeth! Macbeth!

MACBETH
If I had three ears I could hear you more.

Second Apparition
Be violent, bold and stubborn; laugh at the
power of men because no one that has been
born of a woman can hurt Macbeth.

Descends

MACBETH
Then let Macduff live, what do I have to fear
from him?
But, nevertheless, I'll make doubly sure and
swear upon my life that Macduff will not live.
That way, I can rest my fears and sleep well at
night.

*Thunder. Third apparition: a Child crowned,
with a tree in his hand*

What is this that looks like the young son of a
king and wears a crown upon his head?

ALL
Listen but don't talk to it.

Third Apparition
Be lion-mettled, proud; and take no care
Who chafes, who frets, or where conspirers
are:
Macbeth shall never vanquish'd be until
Great Birnam wood to high Dunsinane hill
Shall come against him.

Descends

MACBETH
That will never be
Who can impress the forest, bid the tree
Unfix his earth-bound root? Sweet bodements!
good!
Rebellion's head, rise never till the wood
Of Birnam rise, and our high-placed Macbeth
Shall live the lease of nature, pay his breath
To time and mortal custom. Yet my heart
Throbs to know one thing: tell me, if your art
Can tell so much: shall Banquo's issue ever
Reign in this kingdom?

ALL
Seek to know no more.

MACBETH
I will be satisfied: deny me this,
And an eternal curse fall on you! Let me know.
Why sinks that cauldron? and what noise is
this?

Hautboys

First Witch
Show!

Second Witch
Show!

Third Witch
Show!

ALL
Show his eyes, and grieve his heart;
Come like shadows, so depart!

*A show of Eight Kings, the last with a glass in
his hand; GHOST OF BANQUO following*

Third Apparition
Have the courage of a lion and pay no attention
to those who worry or fret or plot against you:
Macbeth can never be defeated until Great
Birnam Wood marches to Dunsinane Hill.

Descends

MACBETH
That will never happen. Who has such control
over the forest that they can make the tree pick
up its roots from the ground? These are good
tidings! Good! Rebellion against me won't rise
until Birnam Wood does and I will live to be
King for the rest of my natural life.

But my heart aches to know one more thing.
Tell me, if you can, will Banquo's children ever
be kings in Scotland?

ALL
Don't ask anything else.

MACBETH
I demand you answer me: deny me and let an
eternal curse fall on you all!
Let me know!
Why is the cauldron sinking? And what is that
music?

Hautboys

First Witch
Show!

Second Witch
Show!

Third Witch
Show!

ALL
Show him and let it upset him;
Come like shadows and leave in the same way.

*A show of eight Kings, the last with a glass in
his hand; Ghost of BANQUO following*

MACBETH
Thou art too like the spirit of Banquo: down!

Thy crown does sear mine eye-balls. And thy hair,
Thou other gold-bound brow, is like the first.
A third is like the former. Filthy hags!
Why do you show me this? A fourth! Start, eyes!
What, will the line stretch out to the crack of doom?
Another yet! A seventh! I'll see no more:
And yet the eighth appears, who bears a glass
Which shows me many more; and some I see
That two-fold balls and treble scepters carry:
Horrible sight! Now, I see, 'tis true;
For the blood-bolter'd Banquo smiles upon me,
And points at them for his.

Apparitions vanish

What, is this so?

First Witch
Ay, sir, all this is so: but why
Stands Macbeth thus amazedly?
Come, sisters, cheer we up his sprites,
And show the best of our delights:
I'll charm the air to give a sound,
While you perform your antic round:
That this great king may kindly say,
Our duties did his welcome pay.

Music. The witches dance and then vanish, with HECATE

MACBETH
Where are they? Gone? Let this pernicious hour
Stand aye accursed in the calendar!
Come in, without there!

Enter LENNOX

LENNOX
What's your grace's will?

MACBETH
You are too much like the ghost of Banquo: down with you!
Your crown burns my eye-balls, your blond hair is just like the hair of the spirit that came before you. This third is just like first two. Filthy hags!
Why did you show me this? A fourth!
My eyes!
What? Will this line of kings stretch out to the end of the world?
Another one? A seventh? I don't want to see any more but still the eighth one appears who carries a mirror in which I can see many more of these apparitions and some of them carry double balls and triple sceptres telling me that they are king of more than one country: horrible sight! Now I see that it is true, they are really the descendents of Banquo because his blood-spattered face is smiling at me and he's pointing at them to show they're his.

Apparitions vanish

What, is this really true?

First Witch
Yes, sir, all of this is true but why are you so surprised?
Come, sisters, let's cheer him up and show him the best of our talents. I'll create a spell to make the air create music while the rest of you dance around for him so that this great king can say that we performed well for him.

Music. The witches dance and then vanish with HECATE

MACBETH
Where are they? Gone? Let this harmful hour stand as a cursed day in the calendar.
Come in, you who is outside!

Enter LENNOX

LENNOX
What does your majesty want me to do?

MACBETH
Saw you the weird sisters?

LENNOX
No, my lord.

MACBETH
Came they not by you?

LENNOX
No, indeed, my lord.

MACBETH
Infected be the air whereon they ride;
And damn'd all those that trust them! I did hear
The galloping of horse: who was't came by?

LENNOX
'Tis two or three, my lord, that bring you word
Macduff is fled to England.

MACBETH
Fled to England!

LENNOX
Ay, my good lord.

MACBETH
Time, thou anticipatest my dread exploits:
The flighty purpose never is o'ertook
Unless the deed go with it; from this moment
The very firstlings of my heart shall be
The firstlings of my hand. And even now,
To crown my thoughts with acts, be it thought
and done:
The castle of Macduff I will surprise;
Seize upon Fife; give to the edge o' the sword
His wife, his babes, and all unfortunate souls
That trace him in his line. No boasting like a
fool;
This deed I'll do before this purpose cool.
But no more sights!--Where are these
gentlemen?
Come, bring me where they are.

Exeunt

MACBETH
Did you see the weird sister?

LENNOX
No, my lord.

MACBETH
Did they not pass by you?

LENNOX
No, indeed, my lord.

MACBETH
The air itself, on which they fly, is infected, and
damned be anyone who trusts them! I heard
horses galloping by: who was it?

LENNOX
It is two or three messengers my lord, that have
come to bring you a message. Macduff has fled
to England.

MACBETH
Fled to England!

LENNOX
Yes, my good lord.

MACBETH
Time, you have anticipated my terrible plans:
unless someone carries out their plans the
second they think of them, time overtakes
them and they never get around to it. From this
moment on, the very second I think or feel
something, I will carry it out there and then.
And I shall begin right this instant by raiding
Macduff's castle, seizing the town of Fife and
killing his wife, his children and anyone else
unfortunate enough to be in line to his
inheritance. No more talking and boasting like a
fool. I'll do this before my resolve weakens. No
more apparitions! Where are the messengers?
Bring them to me.

Exeunt

Act 4 Scene 2

ORIGINAL TEXT	MODERN TRANSLATION
Fife. Macduff's castle.	**Fife. Macduff's castle.**
Enter LADY MACDUFF, her Son, and ROSS	*Enter LADY MACDUFF, her son and ROSS*
LADY MACDUFF What had he done, to make him fly the land?	**LADY MACDUFF** What has he done to make him run away from Scotland?
ROSS You must have patience, madam.	**ROSS** You must be patient, madam.
LADY MACDUFF He had none: His flight was madness: when our actions do not, Our fears do make us traitors.	**LADY MACDUFF** Well he didn't have any patience: Him leaving is crazy. Sometimes, even if we haven't done anything wrong, our fear of what might happen is enough to make us traitors.
ROSS You know not Whether it was his wisdom or his fear.	**ROSS** You don't know whether he left because he was being wise or afraid.
LADY MACDUFF Wisdom! to leave his wife, to leave his babes, His mansion and his titles in a place From whence himself does fly? He loves us not; He wants the natural touch: for the poor wren, The most diminutive of birds, will fight, Her young ones in her nest, against the owl. All is the fear and nothing is the love; As little is the wisdom, where the flight So runs against all reason.	**LADY MACDUFF** Wisdom! To leave his wife and children, his home and his titles in the very place from which he runs away? He couldn't possibly love us, he lacks the instinct to protect his family. Even the little wren, the smallest and least aggressive of all birds will fight against the owl to protect the young ones in her nest. No, this is all about fear and nothing about love and it's nothing to do with wisdom because running away simply doesn't make any sense.
ROSS My dearest coz, I pray you, school yourself: but for your husband, He is noble, wise, judicious, and best knows The fits o' the season. I dare not speak much further; But cruel are the times, when we are traitors And do not know ourselves, when we hold rumour From what we fear, yet know not what we fear,	**ROSS** My dearest relative, I beg you, pull yourself together. As for your husband, he is noble, wise and has good judgement. He best knows what is needed at what time. I do not want to say too much more because these are cruel times we live in when a man can be denounced as a traitor without knowing what it is he has done. We believe in these frightening and terrible rumours without actually knowing what it is we're afraid of. It is like being in a boat at sea in

But float upon a wild and violent sea
Each way and move. I take my leave of you:
Shall not be long but I'll be here again:
Things at the worst will cease, or else climb upward
To what they were before. My pretty cousin,
Blessing upon you!

LADY MACDUFF
Father'd he is, and yet he's fatherless.

ROSS
I am so much a fool, should I stay longer,
It would be my disgrace and your discomfort:

I take my leave at once.

Exit

LADY MACDUFF
Sirrah, your father's dead;
And what will you do now? How will you live?

Son
As birds do, mother.

LADY MACDUFF
What, with worms and flies?

Son
With what I get, I mean; and so do they.

LADY MACDUFF
Poor bird! thou'ldst never fear the net nor lime,
The pitfall nor the gin.

Son
Why should I, mother? Poor birds they are not set for.
My father is not dead, for all your saying.

LADY MACDUFF
Yes, he is dead; how wilt thou do for a father?

Son
Nay, how will you do for a husband?

a storm; we have no control over what's pushing us around, this way and that.
I'll leave you now. It won't be long until I'm here again. Things are at their worst and it can only stop or improve to the way it was before. My lovely cousin, bless you!

LADY MACDUFF
He has a father but yet he is fatherless.

ROSS
I'd be a fool to stay any longer. It would disgrace you and embarrass me because I'll start crying.
I'll leave you at once.

Exit

LADY MACDUFF
Son, your father's dead. What will you do now? How will you live?

Son
As the birds do, Mother.

LADY MACDUFF
What, will you start eating worms and flies?

Son
No I'll live on what I get I mean, like birds do.

LADY MACDUFF
You'd be a poor bird. You wouldn't know enough to stay away from hunters' traps.

Son
What would I have to fear so mother? The hunters wouldn't want me if I were just a poor bird. My father is not dead, you can say it all you want.

LADY MACDUFF
Yes, he is. Now what will you do for a father?

Son
Maybe I should ask what you will do for a husband?

114

LADY MACDUFF
Why, I can buy me twenty at any market.

Son
Then you'll buy 'em to sell again.

LADY MACDUFF
Thou speak'st with all thy wit: and yet, i' faith,
With wit enough for thee.

Son
Was my father a traitor, mother?

LADY MACDUFF
Ay, that he was.

Son
What is a traitor?

LADY MACDUFF
Why, one that swears and lies.

Son
And be all traitors that do so?

LADY MACDUFF
Every one that does so is a traitor, and must be hanged.

Son
And must they all be hanged that swear and lie?

LADY MACDUFF
Every one.

Son
Who must hang them?

LADY MACDUFF
Why, the honest men.

Son
Then the liars and swearers are fools,
for there are liars and swearers enow to beat the honest men and hang up them.

LADY MACDUFF
Why I can buy twenty husbands for myself at any market.

Son
Then you'd be buying them to sell them on again.

LADY MACDUFF
You're speaking with all your wit. It's not much, but it's good enough for a child.

Son
Was my father a traitor, Mother?

LADY MACDUFF
Yes, he was.

Son
What is a traitor?

LADY MACDUFF
Well, it's someone who swears to do something and then doesn't.

Son
And everyone who does that is a traitor?

LADY MACDUFF
Yes, everyone who does that is a traitor and must be hanged.

Son
And everyone who goes against their word must be hanged?

LADY MACDUFF
Every one of them.

Son
Who has to hang them?

LADY MACDUFF
Well, the honest men.

Son
Then those who go against their words are fools because there's enough of them to beat up all the honest men and hang them instead.

LADY MACDUFF
Now, God help thee, poor monkey!
But how wilt thou do for a father?

Son
If he were dead, you'ld weep for
him: if you would not, it were a good sign
that I should quickly have a new father.

LADY MACDUFF
Poor prattler, how thou talk'st!

Enter a Messenger

Messenger
Bless you, fair dame! I am not to you known,
Though in your state of honour I am perfect.
I doubt some danger does approach you nearly:
If you will take a homely man's advice,
Be not found here; hence, with your little ones.
To fright you thus, methinks, I am too savage;
To do worse to you were fell cruelty,
Which is too nigh your person. Heaven preserve
you!
I dare abide no longer.

Exit

LADY MACDUFF
Whither should I fly?
I have done no harm. But I remember now
I am in this earthly world; where to do harm
Is often laudable, to do good sometime
Accounted dangerous folly: why then, alas,
Do I put up that womanly defence,
To say I have done no harm?

Enter Murderers

What are these faces?

First Murderer
Where is your husband?

LADY MACDUFF
I hope, in no place so unsanctified
Where such as thou mayst find him.

First Murderer
He's a traitor.

LADY MACDUFF
God help you, poor monkey! What will you do
for a father?

Son
If he were really dead you'd weep for him. If
you don't weep, it's a good sign that I will soon
have a new father.

LADY MACDUFF
Silly child, how you talk!

Enter a Messenger

Messenger
Bless you fair lady. You do not know me but I'm
aware of who you are.
I think there is some type of danger coming for
you and, if you will take an honest man's
advice, you and your little ones should not be
here when it arrives.
I hate to frighten you like this, maybe I'm
wrong but to not warn you of what is coming
would be a terrible thing. Heaven keep you
safe! I must leave.

Exit

LADY MACDUFF
Where should I go?
I have done no harm to anyone but, thinking
about it now, I live in a world where to do harm
to people is often the thing that gets praised
while doing good can be seen as madness. So
why then, should I put up this womanly
defence saying I'm innocent?

Enter Murderers

Who are these people?

First Murderer
Where is your husband?

LADY MACDUFF
I hope he's nowhere where someone like you
might find him.

First Murderer
He's a traitor.

Son Thou liest, thou shag-hair'd villain!	**Son** You're a liar you shaggy-haired villain!
First Murderer What, you egg!	**First Murderer** What, you little thing!
Stabbing him	*Stabs him*
Young fry of treachery!	Young son of a traitor!
Son He has kill'd me, mother: Run away, I pray you!	**Son** He has killed me, Mother! Run away, I beg you!
Dies	*Dies*
Exit LADY MACDUFF, crying 'Murder!' Exeunt Murderers, following her	*Exit LADY MACDUFF crying 'Murder!'* *Exeunt Murderers following her*

Act 4 Scene 3

ORIGINAL TEXT	MODERN TRANSLATION
England. Before the King's palace.	**England. Before the King's palace.**
Enter MALCOLM and MACDUFF	*Enter MALCOLM and MACDUFF*
MALCOLM Let us seek out some desolate shade, and there Weep our sad bosoms empty.	**MALCOLM** Let us find somewhere shady where we can cry our hearts out together.
MACDUFF Let us rather Hold fast the mortal sword, and like good men Bestride our down-fall'n birthdom: each new morn New widows howl, new orphans cry, new sorrows Strike heaven on the face, that it resounds As if it felt with Scotland and yell'd out Like syllable of dolour.	**MACDUFF** Instead, why don't we hold onto our swords and, like good men, defend the kingdom of our birth: Every morning, new widows howl, new orphans cry and new sorrows slap heaven in the face almost until it is like heaven itself feels Scotland's anguish and pain.
MALCOLM What I believe I'll wail, What know believe, and what I can redress, As I shall find the time to friend, I will. What you have spoke, it may be so perchance. This tyrant, whose sole name blisters our tongues, Was once thought honest: you have loved him well. He hath not touch'd you yet. I am young; but something You may deserve of him through me, and wisdom To offer up a weak poor innocent lamb To appease an angry god.	**MALCOLM** I will have vengeance for whatever I believe to be wrong. And I will believe whatever is true. And I will find time to do this. What you have said may be true. This tyrant, whose name is so terrible that it hurts us to say it, was once thought to be an honest man. You used to love him. He hasn't harmed you yet. I'm young and inexperienced but maybe you are trying to make Macbeth happy by offering me to him as the sacrificial lamb.
MACDUFF I am not treacherous.	**MACDUFF** I'm not a traitor.
MALCOLM But Macbeth is. A good and virtuous nature may recoil In an imperial charge. But I shall crave your pardon; That which you are my thoughts cannot transpose:	**MALCOLM** But Macbeth is. Even a good and virtuous person may give in when they are commanded to do something by the king. But I apologise. Just because I'm afraid that you might be evil, doesn't actually make you so. Angels are still good even though the

118

Angels are bright still, though the brightest fell;
Though all things foul would wear the brows of grace,
Yet grace must still look so.

MACDUFF
I have lost my hopes.

MALCOLM
Perchance even there where I did find my doubts.
Why in that rawness left you wife and child,
Those precious motives, those strong knots of love,
Without leave-taking? I pray you,
Let not my jealousies be your dishonours,
But mine own safeties. You may be rightly just,
Whatever I shall think.

MACDUFF
Bleed, bleed, poor country!
Great tyranny! lay thou thy basis sure,
For goodness dare not cheque thee: wear thou thy wrongs;
The title is affeer'd! Fare thee well, lord:

I would not be the villain that thou think'st
For the whole space that's in the tyrant's grasp,
And the rich East to boot.

MALCOLM
Be not offended:
I speak not as in absolute fear of you.
I think our country sinks beneath the yoke;
It weeps, it bleeds; and each new day a gash
Is added to her wounds: I think withal

There would be hands uplifted in my right;
And here from gracious England have I offer
Of goodly thousands: but, for all this,
When I shall tread upon the tyrant's head,
Or wear it on my sword, yet my poor country
Shall have more vices than it had before,
More suffer and more sundry ways than ever,
By him that shall succeed.

MACDUFF
What should he be?

---

best of them, Lucifer, fell from heaven. Even though bad things look good, I suppose good things must look good too.

MACDUFF
I have lost my hope of getting you to launch an army against Macbeth.

MALCOLM
Maybe you started to lose hope when I started to have doubts about you.
Why, tell me, did you leave your wife and children, the most important things to a man? How could you leave them without you? I beg you, do not let my suspicions count as your dishonours, I do it for my own safety. You may be good and honest regardless of what I think.

MACDUFF
Bleed, bleed, poor country!
Great tyrant, you are safe in the foundations you have laid, because good people are too afraid to try to stop you.
Show off the evil deeds you committed to get where you are because your title is completely safe. Goodbye Malcolm. I wouldn't be the villain that you think I am even if I were offered all of Macbeth's riches and all the riches of the East in exchange.

MALCOLM
Don't be offended, I'm not completely convinced you are a bad person. I think our country sinks beneath the harness of Macbeth's leadership.
It weeps, it bleeds and each new day another wound is added to all the rest.
I think that there would be many people willing to fight for me if I moved against Macbeth. England has offered me thousands of soldiers to fight against him. But, for all of this, when I have my boot upon Macbeth's head or have it hanging from the end of my sword, my poor country shall have even more problems than when Macbeth was King, with the person who comes after him.

MACDUFF
Who are you talking about?

MALCOLM

It is myself I mean: in whom I know
All the particulars of vice so grafted
That, when they shall be open'd, black Macbeth
Will seem as pure as snow, and the poor state
Esteem him as a lamb, being compared
With my confineless harms.

MACDUFF

Not in the legions
Of horrid hell can come a devil more damn'd
In evils to top Macbeth.

MALCOLM

I grant him bloody,
Luxurious, avaricious, false, deceitful,
Sudden, malicious, smacking of every sin
That has a name: but there's no bottom, none,
In my voluptuousness: your wives, your daughters,
Your matrons and your maids, could not fill up
The cistern of my lust, and my desire
All continent impediments would o'erbear
That did oppose my will: better Macbeth
Than such an one to reign.

MACDUFF

Boundless intemperance
In nature is a tyranny; it hath been
The untimely emptying of the happy throne
And fall of many kings. But fear not yet
To take upon you what is yours: you may
Convey your pleasures in a spacious plenty,
And yet seem cold, the time you may so hoodwink.
We have willing dames enough: there cannot be
That vulture in you, to devour so many
As will to greatness dedicate themselves,
Finding it so inclined.

MALCOLM

With this there grows
In my most ill-composed affection such
A stanchless avarice that, were I king,
I should cut off the nobles for their lands,
Desire his jewels and this other's house:
And my more-having would be as a sauce
To make me hunger more; that I should forge
Quarrels unjust against the good and loyal,
Destroying them for wealth.

MALCOLM

I'm talking about myself. I have so many vices that when people see what I'm really like, they'll think Macbeth was pure as snow in comparison and poor Scotland will call him an innocent lamb when compared to my limitless evils.

MACDUFF

Not even in the most horrid part of hell can there be a devil more terrible than Macbeth.

MALCOLM

He's violent, lustful, greedy, false, deceitful, evil and guilty of every sin that has a name but there is no bottom to my sexual desires. No one would be safe, neither your wives, your daughters, your old women nor young could satisfy my lust. My desire would overcome any restraints or anyone who tried to stand in its way.
It would be better for Macbeth to be king than for someone like me.

MACDUFF

This lust you speak of is a sort of tyranny in itself in a man's nature and it has been the downfall of many kings in the past but do not fear to take upon you the crown, which is yours.
When you are king you can satisfy your desires in a private and secret way while all the while looking virtuous and honourable. We have lots of women who would happily submit to you. You cannot be that greedy to go through all of the women who would sleep with the king if they had the chance?

MALCOLM

As well as being full of lust, I'm also incredibly greedy. If I were King I would steal land from the noblemen, I would take jewels from one person and property from the next.
And the more I took, the more I would want and I would create false arguments with all the good and loyal people so that I can destroy them and take their wealth.

MACDUFF
This avarice
Sticks deeper, grows with more pernicious root
Than summer-seeming lust, and it hath been
The sword of our slain kings: yet do not fear;
Scotland hath foisons to fill up your will.
Of your mere own: all these are portable,
With other graces weigh'd.

MALCOLM
But I have none: the king-becoming graces,
As justice, verity, temperance, stableness,
Bounty, perseverance, mercy, lowliness,
Devotion, patience, courage, fortitude,
I have no relish of them, but abound
In the division of each several crime,
Acting it many ways. Nay, had I power, I should
Pour the sweet milk of concord into hell,
Uproar the universal peace, confound
All unity on earth.

MACDUFF
O Scotland, Scotland!

MALCOLM
If such a one be fit to govern, speak:
I am as I have spoken.

MACDUFF
Fit to govern!
No, not to live. O nation miserable,
With an untitled tyrant bloody-scepter'd,
When shalt thou see thy wholesome days again,
Since that the truest issue of thy throne
By his own interdiction stands accursed,
And does blaspheme his breed? Thy royal father
Was a most sainted king: the queen that bore thee,
Oftener upon her knees than on her feet,
Died every day she lived. Fare thee well!
These evils thou repeat'st upon thyself
Have banish'd me from Scotland. O my breast,
Thy hope ends here!

MALCOLM
Macduff, this noble passion,
Child of integrity, hath from my soul

MACDUFF
This greed is more dangerous than your sexual desire because that is something you can grow out of but greed isn't and it has been the downfall of many a king. But don't worry, Scotland has enough jewels and treasures in its royal coffers to satisfy you. All of these bad things are outweighed by your good sides.

MALCOLM
But I don't have any good sides. Those qualities that someone who is to become king should have like justice, honour, patience, stability, determination, mercy, humility, devotion, courage and strength of character – I have none of them. Instead I am filled with a mixture of all vices possible. No, if I was in power, I would disrupt everything so much that peace everywhere would be disrupted and the earth itself would be unsettled.

MACDUFF
Oh Scotland, Scotland!

MALCOLM
If a person as I have described to you is fit to be the king then let me know.

MACDUFF
Fit to govern!
No, you're not fit to live. Oh, Scotland, with a vicious murdering tyrant who has no claim to the throne, when will you again see the good days?
The rightful heir to the throne, by his own admission, is a cursed man and a disgrace to his own family.
Your royal father was a most saintly and good king. The queen that gave birth to you, who was more often on her knees praying than standing up, prepared herself everyday of her life for when she would go to heaven.
Goodbye. These evil things you have told me about yourself have banished me from Scotland forever. Oh my heart, your hope ends here!

MALCOLM
Macduff, the passion you have just shown tells me that you are an honest person and wipes away all the suspicion I previously had. The

Wiped the black scruples, reconciled my thoughts

To thy good truth and honour. Devilish Macbeth
By many of these trains hath sought to win me
Into his power, and modest wisdom plucks me
From over-credulous haste: but God above
Deal between thee and me! for even now
I put myself to thy direction, and
Unspeak mine own detraction, here abjure
The taints and blames I laid upon myself,
For strangers to my nature. I am yet
Unknown to woman, never was forsworn,
Scarcely have coveted what was mine own,
At no time broke my faith, would not betray
The devil to his fellow and delight
No less in truth than life: my first false speaking
Was this upon myself: what I am truly,
Is thine and my poor country's to command:
Whither indeed, before thy here-approach,
Old Siward, with ten thousand warlike men,
Already at a point, was setting forth.
Now we'll together; and the chance of goodness
Be like our warranted quarrel! Why are you silent?

MACDUFF
Such welcome and unwelcome things at once
'Tis hard to reconcile.

Enter a Doctor

MALCOLM
Well; more anon.--Comes the king forth, I pray you?

Doctor
Ay, sir; there are a crew of wretched souls
That stay his cure: their malady convinces
The great assay of art; but at his touch--
Such sanctity hath heaven given his hand--
They presently amend.

MALCOLM
I thank you, doctor.

Exit Doctor

---

devilish Macbeth has tried many tricks to get me under his power and I have to be very careful about who I trust and believe.
But as God is my witness, I put myself under your direction and I will do as you ask. I take back everything I said before about myself. All of these things I said couldn't be further from the truth. I am still a virgin, I've never told a lie in my life. I have barely wanted my own possessions let alone anyone else's. At no time have I broken a promise and I wouldn't even betray the devil himself. In fact, the first false things I've ever said were these lies I told you about myself.

What I really am is now yours and ready to serve our poor country.
Indeed, just before you arrived, Old Siward was making preparations with ten thousand soldiers to march here. Now we'll all set out together to fight Macbeth.

Why are you silent?

MACDUFF
It's difficult to reconcile the two different stories you have told me.

Enter a Doctor

MALCOLM
Well, we can speak more later, (To the Doctor) Is the King coming out?

Doctor
Yes, sir, there are a group of poor, sick people gathering to wait for him.
Their illnesses cannot be understood or cured by medicine but King Edward can heal them just with his touch because of the power given directly to him by heaven.

MALCOLM
Thank you doctor.

Exit Doctor

MACDUFF
What's the disease he means?

MALCOLM
'Tis call'd the evil:
A most miraculous work in this good king;
Which often, since my here-remain in England,
I have seen him do. How he solicits heaven,
Himself best knows: but strangely-visited people,
All swoln and ulcerous, pitiful to the eye,
The mere despair of surgery, he cures,
Hanging a golden stamp about their necks,
Put on with holy prayers: and 'tis spoken,
To the succeeding royalty he leaves
The healing benediction. With this strange virtue,
He hath a heavenly gift of prophecy,
And sundry blessings hang about his throne,
That speak him full of grace.

Enter ROSS

MACDUFF
See, who comes here?

MALCOLM
My countryman; but yet I know him not.

MACDUFF
My ever-gentle cousin, welcome hither.

MALCOLM
I know him now. Good God, betimes remove
The means that makes us strangers!

ROSS
Sir, amen.

MACDUFF
Stands Scotland where it did?

ROSS
Alas, poor country!
Almost afraid to know itself. It cannot
Be call'd our mother, but our grave; where nothing,
But who knows nothing, is once seen to smile;

MACDUFF
What's this disease he talks about?

MALCOLM
It's called 'the evil'. King Edward does miraculous work through touching them which I've seen often in my time here in England. How he is able to do it only he knows but I've seen him cure people with terrible sicknesses, all swollen and covered in ulcers, pitiful to look at, far beyond the help of surgery, he cures them by hanging a gold coin around their necks and saying prayers over them.
They say that those who come after him will also have this gift.

He also has the ability to see into the future and a number of other strange gifts. These things all show that he is a man who has been touched by God.

Enter ROSS

MACDUFF
Look, who's that coming?

MALCOLM
He looks like he's from Scotland but I do not recognise him.

MACDUFF
My good cousin, welcome.

MALCOLM
Oh, I recognise him now. May God change the reason why we've been apart for so long.

ROSS
Sir, hello.

MACDUFF
Is Scotland still the same as when I left it?

ROSS
Oh, our poor country!
It's almost afraid to look at what its become. It cannot be called the place where we were born anymore, it is now the place where we will die. The only people who smile now are the fools who know nothing. The air is full of sighs,

Where sighs and groans and shrieks that rend
the air
Are made, not mark'd; where violent sorrow
seems
A modern ecstasy; the dead man's knell
Is there scarce ask'd for who; and good men's
lives
Expire before the flowers in their caps,
Dying or ere they sicken.

MACDUFF
O, relation
Too nice, and yet too true!

MALCOLM
What's the newest grief?

ROSS
That of an hour's age doth hiss the speaker:
Each minute teems a new one.

MACDUFF
How does my wife?

ROSS
Why, well.

MACDUFF
And all my children?

ROSS
Well too.

MACDUFF
The tyrant has not batter'd at their peace?

ROSS
No; they were well at peace when I did leave
'em.

MACDUFF
But not a niggard of your speech: how goes't?

ROSS
When I came hither to transport the tidings,
Which I have heavily borne, there ran a rumour
Of many worthy fellows that were out;
Which was to my belief witness'd the rather,
For that I saw the tyrant's power a-foot:
Now is the time of help; your eye in Scotland
Would create soldiers, make our women fight,

---

groans and shrieks but no one pays attention
anymore. There is sorrow everywhere. When
the funeral bell rings, no one asks who it is for
anymore. Men are dying before the flowers in
their caps have time to wilt. They are dying
before they even get sick.

MACDUFF
Oh, what you are telling us sounds too dramatic
but also too true!

MALCOLM
What's the most recent bad news?

ROSS
Even after an hour, news is old and replaced
with new bad news.

MACDUFF
How is my wife?

ROSS
Why, well.

MACDUFF
And all of my children?

ROSS
Well, too.

MACDUFF
The tyrant has not disturbed them?

ROSS
No; they were peaceful when I left them.

MACDUFF
Don't hold back your words, how is everything?

ROSS
When I came here to tell you the bad news, I
heard a rumour that there are men gathering
to rebel against Macbeth. I believe this to be
true because I saw Macbeth's army preparing
for battle.
Now is the time when you are most needed in
Scotland. Your presence there would inspire

To doff their dire distresses.

MALCOLM
Be't their comfort
We are coming thither: gracious England hath
Lent us good Siward and ten thousand men;
An older and a better soldier none
That Christendom gives out.

ROSS
Would I could answer
This comfort with the like! But I have words
That would be howl'd out in the desert air,
Where hearing should not latch them.

MACDUFF
What concern they?
The general cause? or is it a fee-grief
Due to some single breast?

ROSS
No mind that's honest
But in it shares some woe; though the main part
Pertains to you alone.

MACDUFF
If it be mine,
Keep it not from me, quickly let me have it.

ROSS
Let not your ears despise my tongue for ever,
Which shall possess them with the heaviest sound
That ever yet they heard.

MACDUFF
Hum! I guess at it.

ROSS
Your castle is surprised; your wife and babes
Savagely slaughter'd: to relate the manner,
Were, on the quarry of these murder'd deer,
To add the death of you.

MALCOLM
Merciful heaven!
What, man! ne'er pull your hat upon your brows;

people to stand up and fight, it would even make our women want to rise up and fight Macbeth to shake off his terrible reign.

MALCOLM
Be comforted then by the fact that we are coming back. The gracious king of England has lent me Siward and ten thousand troops. There is no better soldier in the Christian world than Siward.

ROSS
I wish I could answer this great news with some good news of my own but unfortunately the news I bear should be howled in a desert where no one could hear it.

MACDUFF
What is this news about?
The general state of things in Scotland or is it personal to one person in particular?

ROSS
No honest man could not share some of this grief but the main part is for you alone.

MACDUFF
If it's for me then don't keep it from me, tell me quickly.

ROSS
Don't hate me for the words I'm about to tell you because they are the worst thing you are ever going to hear.

MACDUFF
I can guess what you are about to tell me.

ROSS
Your castle has been raided; your wife and your children have all been slaughtered. If I went into the detail of how they were killed, it would be too much for you and probably kill you too.

MALCOLM
Merciful heaven!

Give sorrow words: the grief that does not speak
Whispers the o'er-fraught heart and bids it break.

MACDUFF
My children too?

ROSS
Wife, children, servants, all
That could be found.

MACDUFF
And I must be from thence!
My wife kill'd too?

ROSS
I have said.

MALCOLM
Be comforted:
Let's make us medicines of our great revenge,
To cure this deadly grief.

MACDUFF
He has no children. All my pretty ones?
Did you say all? O hell-kite! All?
What, all my pretty chickens and their dam
At one fell swoop?

MALCOLM
Dispute it like a man.

MACDUFF
I shall do so;
But I must also feel it as a man:
I cannot but remember such things were,
That were most precious to me. Did heaven look on,
And would not take their part? Sinful Macduff,
They were all struck for thee! naught that I am,
Not for their own demerits, but for mine,
Fell slaughter on their souls. Heaven rest them now!

MALCOLM
Be this the whetstone of your sword: let grief
Convert to anger; blunt not the heart, enrage it.

Don't hide your grief! Express your sorrow. The grief that you keep hidden inside whispers to your heart until it breaks.

MACDUFF
My children have been killed too?

ROSS
Wife, children, servants, everyone that the murderers could find.

MACDUFF
And I had to be here when it happened! They killed my wife too?

ROSS
Yes, as I said.

MALCOLM
Take comfort. We shall make this better by getting revenge on Macbeth.

MACDUFF
He has no children. All of my children are dead? Did you say all of them? Oh that bird of hell! All? Did you say all of my children and my wife in one go?

MALCOLM
Fight it like a man.

MACDUFF
I will but I must also feel it like a man. I cannot help remembering those things that were so precious to me. Did heaven simply look on and do nothing? Sinful Macduff, they were killed because of you! As bad as I am, they were killed because of me, not anything that they did. May they rest in peace now.

MALCOLM
Let this be the stone on which you sharpen your sword. Let grief change into anger and don't let your heart soften it, let it out as pure rage!

MACDUFF

O, I could play the woman with mine eyes
And braggart with my tongue! But, gentle heavens,
Cut short all intermission; front to front
Bring thou this fiend of Scotland and myself;
Within my sword's length set him; if he 'scape,
Heaven forgive him too!

MALCOLM

This tune goes manly.
Come, go we to the king; our power is ready;
Our lack is nothing but our leave; Macbeth
Is ripe for shaking, and the powers above
Put on their instruments. Receive what cheer you may:
The night is long that never finds the day.

Exeunt

MACDUFF

Oh, I could go on like this, weeping like a woman and boasting about how I will avenge my family but let's cut it short. Heaven, bring forward Macbeth so I can face up to him and have him within sword's reach. If he escapes from me then heaven forgive him too.

MALCOLM

Now this sounds like a man talking. Come on, let's go to the king. Our army is ready. We have nothing left to do here but say goodbye. Macbeth is ready to be taken and we'll be acting in God's name.
Cheer up if you can. A new day will come eventually.

Exeunt

ORIGINAL TEXT	MODERN TRANSLATION
Dunsinane. Ante-room in the castle.	**Dunsinane. Ante-room in the castle.**
Enter a Doctor of Physic and a Waiting-Gentlewoman	*Enter a Doctor of physic and a waiting gentlewoman.*
Doctor I have two nights watched with you, but can perceive no truth in your report. When was it she last walked?	**Doctor** I have stayed up with you for two nights now and I still haven't seen anything to back up what you are saying. When was the last time you saw her sleepwalking?
Gentlewoman Since his majesty went into the field, I have seen her rise from her bed, throw her night-gown upon her, unlock her closet, take forth paper, fold it, write upon't, read it, afterwards seal it, and again return to bed; yet all this while in a most fast sleep.	**Gentlewoman** Since Macbeth went to war I have seen her get up out of her bed, throw on her night-gown, unlock the closet and take some paper from it, fold it, write on it, read it, and then seal it and go back to bed. Yet she does all this while fast asleep.
Doctor A great perturbation in nature, to receive at once the benefit of sleep, and do the effects of watching! In this slumbery agitation, besides her walking and other actual performances, what, at any time, have you heard her say?	**Doctor** It takes a great disruption in nature to cause someone to be asleep yet moving around as if they are awake. When she's like this, besides the things that she has done that you've told me about, does she ever say anything?
Gentlewoman That, sir, which I will not report after her.	**Gentlewoman** That's something I cannot tell you sir.
Doctor You may to me: and 'tis most meet you should.	**Doctor** You may say it to me and you really should.
Gentlewoman Neither to you nor any one; having no witness to confirm my speech.	**Gentlewoman** I won't say it to you or anyone else because there is no witness to confirm what I heard.
Enter LADY MACBETH, with a taper	*Enter LADY MACBETH with a taper*

Lo you, here she comes! This is her very guise; and, upon my life, fast asleep. Observe her; stand close.

Doctor
How came she by that light?

Gentlewoman
Why, it stood by her: she has light by her continually; 'tis her command.

Doctor
You see, her eyes are open.

Gentlewoman
Ay, but their sense is shut.

Doctor
What is it she does now? Look, how she rubs her hands.

Gentlewoman
It is an accustomed action with her, to seem thus
washing her hands: I have known her continue in
this a quarter of an hour.

LADY MACBETH
Yet here's a spot.

Doctor
Hark! she speaks: I will set down what comes from
her, to satisfy my remembrance the more strongly.

LADY MACBETH
Out, damned spot! out, I say!--One: two: why, then, 'tis time to do't.--Hell is murky!--Fie, my lord, fie! a soldier, and afeard? What need we fear who knows it, when none can call our power to
account?--Yet who would have thought the old man
to have had so much blood in him.

Doctor
Do you mark that?

Look, here she comes! This is just how she looks and, I swear on my life, she is fast asleep. Look at her, but stay out of sight.

Doctor
Where did she get that candle?

Gentlewoman
It's from the bedside table. She has a light by her at all times. Those are her orders.

Doctor
You see, her eyes are open.

Gentlewoman
Yes but they are not seeing anything.

Doctor
What is she doing now? Look how she rubs her hands.

Gentlewoman
It is a regular thing with her to look as though she is washing her hands. I have seen her do this for quarter of an hour at a time.

LADY MACBETH
There's still a spot.

Doctor
Listen! She is speaking: I will take note of what she says so that I can remember this event more clearly.

LADY MACBETH
Out, damned stain! Come out I say! One, two, now's the time to come out. Hell is murky! Nonsense my lord, nonsense! You're a soldier and you're afraid? Why should we fear anyone when we are in charge and no one can lay the blame on us?
But who would have thought the old man would have had so much blood in him.

Doctor
Did you hear that?

LADY MACBETH
The thane of Fife had a wife: where is she now?--
What, will these hands ne'er be clean?--No more o'
that, my lord, no more o' that: you mar all with this starting.

Doctor
Go to, go to; you have known what you should not.

Gentlewoman
She has spoke what she should not, I am sure of that: heaven knows what she has known.

LADY MACBETH
Here's the smell of the blood still: all the perfumes of Arabia will not sweeten this little hand. Oh, oh, oh!

Doctor
What a sigh is there! The heart is sorely charged.

Gentlewoman
I would not have such a heart in my bosom for the
dignity of the whole body.

Doctor
Well, well, well,--

Gentlewoman
Pray God it be, sir.

Doctor
This disease is beyond my practise: yet I have known
those which have walked in their sleep who have died
holily in their beds.

LADY MACBETH
Wash your hands, put on your nightgown; look not so
pale.--I tell you yet again, Banquo's buried; he cannot come out on's grave.

LADY MACBETH
The thane of Fife had a wife, where is she now? What, will these hands never be clean?
No more of that, my lord, no more of that. You'll spoil it all by acting so startled.

Doctor
Alas! You have heard something you should not have.

Gentlewoman
She has said something she should not have, I am sure of that. God only knows the secrets she has.

LADY MACBETH
I can still smell blood. All the perfumes of Arabia will not sweeten the smell of my hands. Oh, oh, oh!

Doctor
What a sigh that is. There is something weighing very heavily on her heart.

Gentlewoman
I wouldn't have a heart like hers even if you made me the queen.

Doctor
Well, well, well.

Gentlewoman
I hope what she's saying is well sir.

Doctor
This disease is outside of my expertise but I've known people who have been afflicted by sleepwalking and they never committed any crimes.

LADY MACBETH
Wash your hands and put on your night-gown. Don't look so pale. I tell you once again, Banquo's dead and buried, he cannot come out of his own grave.

Doctor
Even so?

LADY MACBETH
To bed, to bed! there's knocking at the gate:
come, come, come, come, give me your hand. What's
done cannot be undone.--To bed, to bed, to bed!

Exit

Doctor
Will she go now to bed?

Gentlewoman
Directly.

Doctor
Foul whisperings are abroad: unnatural deeds
Do breed unnatural troubles: infected minds
To their deaf pillows will discharge their secrets:
More needs she the divine than the physician.
God, God forgive us all! Look after her;
Remove from her the means of all annoyance,
And still keep eyes upon her. So, good night:
My mind she has mated, and amazed my sight.
I think, but dare not speak.

Gentlewoman
Good night, good doctor.

Exeunt

Doctor
Is this true?

LADY MACBETH
To bed, to bed! There's a knocking at the gate:
come, come, come, come. Give me your hand.
What's done cannot be undone. To bed, to bed, to bed!

Exit

Doctor
Will she go to bed now?

Gentlewoman
Directly.

Doctor
There are some evil rumours going around:
unnatural acts cause unnatural troubles for
people. Damaged minds sometimes confess
their secrets to their pillows.
She needs a priest more than a doctor.
God, God forgive us all! Look after her and take
away from her anything that she could use to
hurt herself and watch over her.
So good night, I'm amazed at what I've seen
this evening. I have my theories but I dare not
say what they are.

Gentlewoman
Good night, good doctor.

Exeunt

ORIGINAL TEXT	MODERN TRANSLATION
The country near Dunsinane.	**The country near Dunsinane.**
Drum and colours. Enter MENTEITH, CAITHNESS, ANGUS, LENNOX, and Soldiers	*Drum and colours. Enter MENTEITH, CAITHNESS, ANGUS, LENNOX and soldiers*
MENTEITH The English power is near, led on by Malcolm, His uncle Siward and the good Macduff: Revenges burn in them; for their dear causes Would to the bleeding and the grim alarm Excite the mortified man.	**MENTEITH** The English army is nearby, led by Malcolm, his uncle Siward and the good Macduff. Revenge burns in them. Their different causes would be enough to make dead mean rise up and fight.
ANGUS Near Birnam wood Shall we well meet them; that way are they coming.	**ANGUS** Near Birnam wood we'll meet them. They are coming that way.
CAITHNESS Who knows if Donalbain be with his brother?	**CAITHNESS** Does anyone know if Donalbain is with his brother Malcolm?
LENNOX For certain, sir, he is not: I have a file Of all the gentry: there is Siward's son, And many unrough youths that even now Protest their first of manhood.	**LENNOX** No, definitely not sir. I have a file on all of the noblemen in the group: there is Siward's son, and many boys, too young yet to have beards but who will beome men in this battle.
MENTEITH What does the tyrant?	**MENTEITH** What's Macbeth doing?
CAITHNESS Great Dunsinane he strongly fortifies: Some say he's mad; others that lesser hate him Do call it valiant fury: but, for certain, He cannot buckle his distemper'd cause Within the belt of rule.	**CAITHNESS** He's fortifying his castle at Dunsinane. Some people say he's gone crazy, others that don't hate him as much say it's courageous fury. One thing's for certain though, he's lost all control.
ANGUS Now does he feel His secret murders sticking on his hands; Now minutely revolts upbraid his faith-breach; Those he commands move only in command, Nothing in love: now does he feel his title Hang loose about him, like a giant's robe Upon a dwarfish thief.	**ANGUS** Now he feels the blood from his secret murders sticking to his hands. Now, people are rebelling against him and his army is only fighting because they are commanded to, not because they love him. Now his title of king doesn't fit him. It's as if he's wearing the robes of a giant but he's only a dwarfish thief.

MENTEITH Who then shall blame His pester'd senses to recoil and start, When all that is within him does condemn Itself for being there? **CAITHNESS** Well, march we on, To give obedience where 'tis truly owed: Meet we the medicine of the sickly weal, And with him pour we in our country's purge Each drop of us. **LENNOX** Or so much as it needs, To dew the sovereign flower and drown the weeds. Make we our march towards Birnam. *Exeunt, marching*	**MENTEITH** Who can blame him for being unstable and out of control when inside, he blames himself for everything that he's done. **CAITHNESS** Well, let's march on and give our loyalty to someone who truly deserves it. Let's meet Malcolm, the doctor who will cure this sick country and we will pour out our own blood to help him do it. **LENNOX** Or as much as he needs to help the royal flower grow and drown the weeds. Come, let's march to Birnam. *Exeunt, marching*

ORIGINAL TEXT	MODERN TRANSLATION
Dunsinane. A room in the castle.	**Dunsinane. A room in the castle.**
Enter MACBETH, Doctor, and Attendants	*Enter MACBETH, Doctor and attendants*
MACBETH Bring me no more reports; let them fly all: Till Birnam wood remove to Dunsinane, I cannot taint with fear. What's the boy Malcolm? Was he not born of woman? The spirits that know All mortal consequences have pronounced me thus: 'Fear not, Macbeth; no man that's born of woman Shall e'er have power upon thee.' Then fly, false thanes, And mingle with the English epicures: The mind I sway by and the heart I bear Shall never sag with doubt nor shake with fear.	**MACBETH** Don't bring me any more news. I don't care if they all desert me! Until Birnam wood moves to Dunsinane, I cannot be afraid of anything? What's the boy Malcolm? Was he not born from a woman? The witches, who can see into the future, told me: "Fear not, Macbeth, no man that's born from a woman can ever harm you." Then fly, false lords, and go join the indulgent English, my mind and my courage will never be affected by doubt nor shake with fear.
Enter a Servant	*Enter a Servant*
The devil damn thee black, thou cream-faced loon! Where got'st thou that goose look?	May the devil turn you black you pale-faced idiot! Why have you got such a startled look on your face?
Servant There is ten thousand--	**Servant** There is ten thousand…
MACBETH Geese, villain!	**MACBETH** Geese, you fool?
Servant Soldiers, sir.	**Servant** Soldiers, sir.
MACBETH Go prick thy face, and over-red thy fear, Thou lily-liver'd boy. What soldiers, patch? Death of thy soul! those linen cheeks of thine Are counsellors to fear. What soldiers, whey-face?	**MACBETH** Go and pinch your cheeks to bring some colour back into your face, you coward. What soldiers, clown? Death to your soul! Those pale cheeks of yours will spread fear to the others. What soldiers, milk-face?

Servant
The English force, so please you.

MACBETH
Take thy face hence.

Exit Servant

Seyton!--I am sick at heart,
When I behold--Seyton, I say!--This push
Will cheer me ever, or disseat me now.
I have lived long enough: my way of life
Is fall'n into the sear, the yellow leaf;
And that which should accompany old age,
As honour, love, obedience, troops of friends,
I must not look to have; but, in their stead,
Curses, not loud but deep, mouth-honour, breath,
Which the poor heart would fain deny, and dare not. Seyton!

Enter SEYTON

SEYTON
What is your gracious pleasure?

MACBETH
What news more?

SEYTON
All is confirm'd, my lord, which was reported.

MACBETH
I'll fight till from my bones my flesh be hack'd.
Give me my armour.

SEYTON
'Tis not needed yet.

MACBETH
I'll put it on.
Send out more horses; skirr the country round;
Hang those that talk of fear. Give me mine armour.
How does your patient, doctor?

Doctor
Not so sick, my lord,
As she is troubled with thick coming fancies,
That keep her from her rest.

Servant
The English army, sir.

MACBETH
Get out of my sight.

Exit Servant

Seyton! My heart is sick when I see – Seyton, come here! – this battle will either cement my place forever or force me from the throne.
I have lived long enough. Now my life passes into its autumnal stage like a yellowing leaf and all those things that should accompany old age like honour, love, obedience, lots of friends, I can't hope to have. Instead, I have quiet but passionate curses, people who honour me with their words but not with their hearts. I would gladly end this lingering life but I dare not. Seyton!

Enter SEYTON

SEYTON
What would you like, your majesty?

MACBETH
Is there any more news?

SEYTON
All the rumours and talk have been confirmed my lord.

MACBETH
I'll fight them until the flesh is hacked from my bones. Give me my armour.

SEYTON
There's no need for it yet.

MACBETH
I'll put it on anyway. Send out more men on horseback. Scour the countryside and hang anyone who is spreading fear. Give me my armour. How is my wife, doctor?

Doctor
Not as sick as she is troubled, my lord, by visions that keep her from sleeping properly.

MACBETH
Cure her of that.
Canst thou not minister to a mind diseased,
Pluck from the memory a rooted sorrow,
Raze out the written troubles of the brain
And with some sweet oblivious antidote
Cleanse the stuff'd bosom of that perilous stuff
Which weighs upon the heart?

Doctor
Therein the patient
Must minister to himself.

MACBETH
Throw physic to the dogs; I'll none of it.

Come, put mine armour on; give me my staff.
Seyton, send out. Doctor, the thanes fly from
me.
Come, sir, dispatch. If thou couldst, doctor, cast
The water of my land, find her disease,
And purge it to a sound and pristine health,
I would applaud thee to the very echo,
That should applaud again.--Pull't off, I say.--
What rhubarb, cyme, or what purgative drug,
Would scour these English hence? Hear'st thou
of them?

Doctor
Ay, my good lord; your royal preparation
Makes us hear something.

MACBETH
Bring it after me.
I will not be afraid of death and bane,
Till Birnam forest come to Dunsinane.

Doctor
[Aside] Were I from Dunsinane away and clear,
Profit again should hardly draw me here.

Exeunt

MACBETH
Cure her of it. Can you not treat a damaged
mind?
Take, from the memory, a deeply buried
sorrow, erase the troubles written on the brain
and with some sort of medicine remove the
problems that weigh heavily upon her heart?

Doctor
Unfortunately, that is something that has to
come from the patient herself.

MACBETH
Throw medicine to the dogs, I'll have no more
of it.
Come, put on my armour; give me my staff.
Seyton, let's go. Doctor, the lords are running
from me to the English. Can you search the
waters of Scotland and find what disease is
affecting the country? If you could cleanse the
water of that disease and make it clean again,
I'd applaud you to the ends of the earth so that
it would echo back and you would hear it again.
Pull it off, Seyton!
Doctor, is there any drug that could cleanse our
lands of the English? Have you heard of
anything that could do it?

Doctor
Yes, my good lord, the battle that you are
preparing for sounds like something.

MACBETH
Seyton, bring it with you and follow me. I will
not be afraid of death until Birnam forest
marches on Dunsinane.

Doctor
[Aside] I wish I were as far away from
Dunsinane as possible. I will never come back
here again, not even for money.
Exeunt

Act 5 Scene 4

ORIGINAL TEXT	MODERN TRANSLATION
Country near Birnam wood.	**Country near Birnam wood.**
Drum and colours. Enter MALCOLM, SIWARD and YOUNG SIWARD, MACDUFF, MENTEITH, CAITHNESS, ANGUS, LENNOX, ROSS, and Soldiers, marching	*Drum and colours. Enter MALCOLM, SIWARD and YOUNG SIWARD, MACDUFF, MENTEITH, CAITHNESS, ANGUS, LENNOX, ROSS and soldiers marching.*
MALCOLM Cousins, I hope the days are near at hand That chambers will be safe.	**MALCOLM** Kinsmen, I hope the day will soon be here when people will be able to sleep safely in their own beds.
MENTEITH We doubt it nothing.	**MENTEITH** We don't doubt it.
SIWARD What wood is this before us?	**SIWARD** What is this wood in front of us?
MENTEITH The wood of Birnam.	**MENTEITH** The wood of Birnam.
MALCOLM Let every soldier hew him down a bough And bear't before him: thereby shall we shadow The numbers of our host and make discovery Err in report of us.	**MALCOLM** Tell every soldier to cut down a branch and carry it in front of him as we march. That way, we can hide the true number of soldiers we have and Macbeth's spies will give him inaccurate reports.
Soldiers It shall be done.	**Soldiers** It shall be done.
SIWARD We learn no other but the confident tyrant Keeps still in Dunsinane, and will endure Our setting down before 't.	**SIWARD** We've heard nothing other than Macbeth, being confident of victory, remains in his castle in Dunsinane and will not stop us from marching to it.
MALCOLM 'Tis his main hope: For where there is advantage to be given, Both more and less have given him the revolt, And none serve with him but constrained things Whose hearts are absent too.	**MALCOLM** He wants us to lay siege to it. Whenever his soldiers have a chance to leave him, they do, and no one remains fighting with him only those who have to and their hearts are not in it.

MACDUFF Let our just censures Attend the true event, and put we on Industrious soldiership. **SIWARD** The time approaches That will with due decision make us know What we shall say we have and what we owe. Thoughts speculative their unsure hopes relate, But certain issue strokes must arbitrate: Towards which advance the war. *Exeunt, marching*	**MACDUFF** Let's not make any judgements now. Let's just get on with the work like good soldiers. **SIWARD** The time approaches when we will find out what's ours and what is not. Guessing and supposing, it's easy to get our hopes up just sitting here but nothing will be decided without violence so let's move our army forward. *Exeunt, marching*

Act 5 Scene 5

ORIGINAL TEXT	MODERN TRANSLATION
Dunsinane. Within the castle.	**DUNSINANE. Within the castle.**
Enter MACBETH, SEYTON, and Soldiers, with drum and colours	*Enter MACBETH, SEYTON and soldiers with drums and colours*
MACBETH Hang out our banners on the outward walls; The cry is still 'They come:' our castle's strength Will laugh a siege to scorn: here let them lie Till famine and the ague eat them up: Were they not forced with those that should be ours, We might have met them dareful, beard to beard, And beat them backward home.	**MACBETH** Hang our banners on the outer walls of the castle; The cry from everyone is still "They come". Our castle's strength will laugh at their forces. Let them lie outside the castle walls until famine and disease kill them. If it wasn't for the fact that so many of our own soldiers have joined their ranks, we'd have gone out and met them beard to beard on the battlefield and beat them.
A cry of women within	*A cry of women within*
What is that noise?	What is that noise?
SEYTON It is the cry of women, my good lord.	**SEYTON** It is the cry of women, my good lord.
Exit	*Exit*
MACBETH I have almost forgot the taste of fears; The time has been, my senses would have cool'd To hear a night-shriek; and my fell of hair Would at a dismal treatise rouse and stir As life were in't: I have supp'd full with horrors; Direness, familiar to my slaughterous thoughts Cannot once start me.	**MACBETH** I have almost forgotten what it is like to be afraid. There was a time when I would have been terrified to hear a shriek in the night and my hair would stand on end upon hearing a simple ghost story. But now, I have become so accustomed to horrors that they cannot frighten me any longer.
Re-enter SEYTON	*Re-enter SEYTON*
Wherefore was that cry?	What was that cry for?
SEYTON The queen, my lord, is dead.	**SEYTON** The queen is dead, my lord.

MACBETH

She should have died hereafter;
There would have been a time for such a word.
To-morrow, and to-morrow, and to-morrow,
Creeps in this petty pace from day to day
To the last syllable of recorded time,
And all our yesterdays have lighted fools
The way to dusty death. Out, out, brief candle!
Life's but a walking shadow, a poor player
That struts and frets his hour upon the stage
And then is heard no more: it is a tale
Told by an idiot, full of sound and fury,
Signifying nothing.

Enter a Messenger
Thou comest to use thy tongue; thy story
quickly.

Messenger
Gracious my lord,
I should report that which I say I saw,
But know not how to do it.

MACBETH
Well, say, sir.

Messenger
As I did stand my watch upon the hill,
I look'd toward Birnam, and anon, methought,
The wood began to move.

MACBETH
Liar and slave!

Messenger
Let me endure your wrath, if't be not so:
Within this three mile may you see it coming;
I say, a moving grove.

MACBETH
If thou speak'st false,
Upon the next tree shalt thou hang alive,
Till famine cling thee: if thy speech be sooth,
I care not if thou dost for me as much.
I pull in resolution, and begin
To doubt the equivocation of the fiend
That lies like truth: 'Fear not, till Birnam wood
Do come to Dunsinane:' and now a wood
Comes toward Dunsinane. Arm, arm, and out!
If this which he avouches does appear,
There is nor flying hence nor tarrying here.

MACBETH

She would have died sometime anyway. That news was always going to come.
Tomorrow and tomorrow and tomorrow, creeps up on us day after day until the very end of time, and every day that we spend along the way simply bring us closer to our deaths.
Out, out brief candle! Life's but an illusion, a poor actor that struts and worries about his hour on the stage and then is never heard from again. Life is just a tale told by an idiot full of sounds and emotions but actually meaning nothing in the end.

Enter a Messenger

You came to tell me something; what is it?

Messenger
Gracious my lord,
I should tell you what I've seen but I do not know how to begin.

MACBETH
Just tell me.

Messenger
As I stood watch on the hill, I looked towards Birnam Wood and I thought I saw the wood begin to move.

MACBETH
Liar and slave!

Messenger
You can punish me if what I've said isn't true. Just three miles away, you can see it coming, like I've said, a moving grove of trees.

MACBETH
If you are lying I will hang you alive from the nearest tree until you starve to death. If what you say is true then you may do the same to me.
My belief in what the devil told me through those witches is beginning to falter. They told me "Don't be afraid until Birnam wood comes to Dunsinane" and now a wood is coming towards Dunsinane. Let's prepare for battle!
If the messenger is correct, there is no point in running away or waiting here in the castle.

I gin to be aweary of the sun, And wish the estate o' the world were now undone. Ring the alarum-bell! Blow, wind! come, wrack! At least we'll die with harness on our back. *Exeunt*	I'm beginning to grow weary of life, and I want to see the world turned upside down in chaos. Ring the alarm bell! Blow, wind! Come destruction! At least we'll die with our armour on. *Exeunt*

ORIGINAL TEXT	MODERN TRANSLATION
Dunsinane. Before the castle.	**Dunsinane. Before the castle.**
Drum and colours. Enter MALCOLM, SIWARD, MACDUFF, and their Army, with boughs	*Drum and colours. Enter MALCOLM, SIWARD, MACDUFF and their army with branches*
MALCOLM Now near enough: your leafy screens throw down. And show like those you are. You, worthy uncle, Shall, with my cousin, your right-noble son, Lead our first battle: worthy Macduff and we Shall take upon 's what else remains to do, According to our order.	**MALCOLM** Now we're near enough. Throw down your branches and show them our true numbers. You, Siward, shall, with your good son, lead the first charge. Macduff and I will take up the rest according to our battle plan.
SIWARD Fare you well. Do we but find the tyrant's power to-night, Let us be beaten, if we cannot fight.	**SIWARD** Good luck. If we meet the tyrant's army tonight, let us be beaten if we cannot fight.
MACDUFF Make all our trumpets speak; give them all breath, Those clamorous harbingers of blood and death.	**MACDUFF** Sound all the trumpets, they are the signal for blood and death.
Exeunt	*Exeunt*

Act 5 Scene 7

ORIGINAL TEXT	MODERN TRANSLATION
Another part of the field.	**Another part of the field.**
Alarums. Enter MACBETH	*Alarms. Enter MACBETH*
MACBETH They have tied me to a stake; I cannot fly, But, bear-like, I must fight the course. What's he That was not born of woman? Such a one Am I to fear, or none.	**MACBETH** They have tied me to a stake and I cannot leave but, like a bear, I must stand and fight to the death. Where's the man not born from a woman? He is the only one I'm afraid of.
Enter YOUNG SIWARD	*Enter YOUNG SIWARD*
YOUNG SIWARD What is thy name?	**YOUNG SIWARD** What is your name?
MACBETH Thou'lt be afraid to hear it.	**MACBETH** You would be afraid to hear it.
YOUNG SIWARD No; though thou call'st thyself a hotter name Than any is in hell.	**YOUNG SIWARD** No. Even if you call yourself a worse name than any in hell.
MACBETH My name's Macbeth.	**MACBETH** My name's Macbeth.
YOUNG SIWARD The devil himself could not pronounce a title More hateful to mine ear.	**YOUNG SIWARD** The devil himself could not say a name I hate more than that.
MACBETH No, nor more fearful.	**MACBETH** No, he couldn't say one you're more afraid of either.
YOUNG SIWARD Thou liest, abhorred tyrant; with my sword I'll prove the lie thou speak'st.	**YOUNG SIWARD** You're a liar, terrible tyrant, with my sword I'll prove you are a liar.
They fight and YOUNG SIWARD is slain	*They fight and YOUNG SIWARD is slain*
MACBETH Thou wast born of woman But swords I smile at, weapons laugh to scorn, Brandish'd by man that's of a woman born.	**MACBETH** You were born from a woman. I smile at swords, laugh at weapons that are held by men born from women.
Exit	*Exit*

Alarums. Enter MACDUFF	*Alarms. Enter MACDUFF*
MACDUFF That way the noise is. Tyrant, show thy face! If thou be'st slain and with no stroke of mine, My wife and children's ghosts will haunt me still. I cannot strike at wretched kerns, whose arms Are hired to bear their staves: either thou, Macbeth, Or else my sword with an unbatter'd edge I sheathe again undeeded. There thou shouldst be; By this great clatter, one of greatest note Seems bruited. Let me find him, fortune! And more I beg not.	**MACDUFF** The noise is over there. Tyrant, show your face! If someone other than me kills you the ghosts of my wife and children will haunt me forever. I cannot fight these soldiers who only fight for money. Either I fight you, Macbeth, or I will put down my sword unused. There, that's where you are! By the great noise, it sounds like one of the more important people are being announced. Please let me find him! I do not ask for anything else.
Exit. Alarums	*Exit. Alarms*
Enter MALCOLM and SIWARD	*Enter MALCOLM and SIWARD*
SIWARD This way, my lord; the castle's gently render'd: The tyrant's people on both sides do fight; The noble thanes do bravely in the war; The day almost itself professes yours, And little is to do.	**SIWARD** This way, my lord, the castle has been surrendered with no trouble. Macbeth's soldiers fight on both sides and the noblemen are fighting bravely. The day is almost won and victory is nearly yours.
MALCOLM We have met with foes That strike beside us.	**MALCOLM** it's almost as if the soldiers fighting for Macbeth don't want to hurt us.
SIWARD Enter, sir, the castle.	**SIWARD** Enter the castle, sir.
Exeunt. Alarums	*Exeunt. Alarms*

Act 5 Scene 8

ORIGINAL TEXT	MODERN TRANSLATION
Another part of the field.	**Another part of the field.**
Enter MACBETH	*Enter MACBETH*
MACBETH Why should I play the Roman fool, and die On mine own sword? whiles I see lives, the gashes Do better upon them.	**MACBETH** Why should I be like one of those foolish Romans and kill myself with my own sword? While I still see my enemies alive, I would prefer to kill them than they kill me.
Enter MACDUFF	*Enter MACDUFF*
MACDUFF Turn, hell-hound, turn!	**MACDUFF** Turn, you dog of hell, turn!
MACBETH Of all men else I have avoided thee: But get thee back; my soul is too much charged With blood of thine already.	**MACBETH** You are the one man I have avoided. But go away from here, I have already killed your family, I have your blood on my soul.
MACDUFF I have no words: My voice is in my sword: thou bloodier villain Than terms can give thee out!	**MACDUFF** I have no words for you. I'll let my sword speak for me. You are too evil for words.
They fight	*They fight*
MACBETH Thou losest labour: As easy mayst thou the intrenchant air With thy keen sword impress as make me bleed: Let fall thy blade on vulnerable crests; I bear a charmed life, which must not yield, To one of woman born.	**MACBETH** You are wasting your efforts. You would have as much luck cutting at the air with your sword than making me bleed. You should fight someone who can be harmed. I am charmed and cannot be killed by anyone born from a woman.
MACDUFF Despair thy charm; And let the angel whom thou still hast served Tell thee, Macduff was from his mother's womb Untimely ripp'd.	**MACDUFF** Forget about your charms and let the spirit you serve tell you, Macduff was, from him mother's womb, cut out before she gave birth.
MACBETH Accursed be that tongue that tells me so, For it hath cow'd my better part of man!	**MACBETH** Damn you for telling me this because it has taken away all my courage!

And be these juggling fiends no more believed, That palter with us in a double sense; That keep the word of promise to our ear, And break it to our hope. I'll not fight with thee.	I no longer believe the evil creatures who have tricked me with their words and double meanings that have raised my hopes and then destroyed them. I will not fight you.
MACDUFF Then yield thee, coward, And live to be the show and gaze o' the time: We'll have thee, as our rarer monsters are, Painted on a pole, and underwrit, 'Here may you see the tyrant.'	**MACDUFF** Then surrender, coward. And spend the rest of your days in a travelling show. We'll put you, like rare monsters, in a cage and painted on a pole before it will say "Here you may see the tyrant".
MACBETH I will not yield, To kiss the ground before young Malcolm's feet, And to be baited with the rabble's curse. Though Birnam wood be come to Dunsinane, And thou opposed, being of no woman born, Yet I will try the last. Before my body I throw my warlike shield. Lay on, Macduff, And damn'd be him that first cries, 'Hold, enough!'	**MACBETH** I will not give up, to kiss the ground beneath young Malcolm's feet and to be taunted and mocked by common people. Even though Birnam wood came to Dunsinane and you are not from woman born, I'll keep fighting to the last. I'll put my shield up in front of me. Come on Macduff and damned be the first man to cry 'stop!'
Exeunt, fighting. Alarums	*Exeunt, fighting, Alarms*
Retreat. Flourish. Enter, with drum and colours, MALCOLM, SIWARD, ROSS, the other Thanes, and Soldiers	*Retreat. Flourish. Enter, with a drum and colours, MALCOLM, SIWARD, ROSS, the other lords and soldiers*

Act 5 Scene 9

ORIGINAL TEXT	MODERN TRANSLATION
MALCOLM I would the friends we miss were safe arrived.	**MALCOLM** I wish our friends could have survived this battle.
SIWARD Some must go off: and yet, by these I see, So great a day as this is cheaply bought.	**SIWARD** Some people must die in every battle and still, by looking at the men around me, I don't think that our great victory cost us too much.
MALCOLM Macduff is missing, and your noble son.	**MALCOLM** Macduff is missing and your noble son, Young Siward.
ROSS Your son, my lord, has paid a soldier's debt: He only lived but till he was a man; The which no sooner had his prowess confirm'd In the unshrinking station where he fought, But like a man he died.	**ROSS** Your son, my lord, has paid the ultimate price of being a soldier: death. He only lived until he was barely a man but he proved he was a man by the way he fought and died.
SIWARD Then he is dead?	**SIWARD** So he is dead?
ROSS Ay, and brought off the field: your cause of sorrow Must not be measured by his worth, for then It hath no end.	**ROSS** Yes and his body has been brought from the battle field. Your sorrow must not be equal to his worth, otherwise you would never stop grieving for him.
SIWARD Had he his hurts before?	**SIWARD** Were his wounds to his front?
ROSS Ay, on the front.	**ROSS** Yes, on the front.
SIWARD Why then, God's soldier be he! Had I as many sons as I have hairs, I would not wish them to a fairer death: And so, his knell is knoll'd.	**SIWARD** Well then, he's God's soldier now. If I had as many sons as I do hairs, I could not wish them a more honourable death than he had so that's it.
MALCOLM He's worth more sorrow, And that I'll spend for him.	**MALCOLM** He's worth more mourning than that and I will mourn for him.

SIWARD
He's worth no more
They say he parted well, and paid his score:
And so, God be with him! Here comes newer comfort.

Re-enter MACDUFF, with MACBETH's head

MACDUFF
Hail, king! for so thou art: behold, where stands
The usurper's cursed head: the time is free:

I see thee compass'd with thy kingdom's pearl,
That speak my salutation in their minds;
Whose voices I desire aloud with mine:
Hail, King of Scotland!

ALL
Hail, King of Scotland!

Flourish

MALCOLM
We shall not spend a large expense of time
Before we reckon with your several loves,
And make us even with you. My thanes and kinsmen,
Henceforth be earls, the first that ever Scotland
In such an honour named. What's more to do,
Which would be planted newly with the time,
As calling home our exiled friends abroad
That fled the snares of watchful tyranny;
Producing forth the cruel ministers
Of this dead butcher and his fiend-like queen,
Who, as 'tis thought, by self and violent hands
Took off her life; this, and what needful else
That calls upon us, by the grace of Grace,
We will perform in measure, time and place:
So, thanks to all at once and to each one,
Whom we invite to see us crown'd at Scone.

Flourish. Exeunt

SIWARD
He's worth no more. They have said that he died well and paid his price and so, God be with him!
Here comes good news.

Re-enter MACDUFF, with MACBETH'S head

MACDUFF
Hail, King! For that is what you now are. Here I have Macbeth's cursed head, we are free of him.
I see that you've all the best noblemen of Scotland standing around you and we're all thinking the same thing so let's join together in a loud cheer:
Hail, King of Scotland!

ALL
Hail, King of Scotland!

Flourish

MALCOLM
It won't be long before I reward all of you for your honour and loyalty. My lords and kingsmen, I name you all Earls, the first Earls that Scotland has had.
We have much to do at this new beginning for our country.
We must call home all our exiled friends who fled the watchful traps of Macbeth and we must bring to justice all of the evil people who worked with this dead butcher and his evil queen who, according to rumour, has killed herself. This and anything else God requires us to do will be done in the right time and place.
So I thank each and every one of you and I invite you all to come and watch me be crowned at Scone.

Flourish. Exeunt

Printed in Great Britain
by Amazon